BY GRACE THROUGH

FAITH

A JOURNEY OF SELF-DISCOVERY

By Grace Through Faith

A JOURNEY OF SELF-DISCOVERY

Copyright © 2022 Jared Nicholas Demarco McPhoy

All scripture references used in this book were taken from the Holy Bible, Common English Version and can be found at http://thebiblegateway.com.

Editor: Crystal S. Wright

ISBN: 979-8-9860947-9-3

10 9 8 7 6 5 4 3 2 1
Printed in the United States

Priceless Publishing®
pricelesspublishing.co
Lauderhill, Florida

This book is dedicated to all the dreamers out there:
Don't forget to dream big.

DREAM AUDACIOUSLY!

It does not matter where you come from.
All things happen for them who believe and work hard.

Table of Contents

*To a fetus under attack when God
sent a word that He has purpose for its life.
This is the moment when purpose comes alive!*

CHAPTER ONE:

In the Beginning There Was Jared

On the 30th of October 1998 the world welcomed the multi-hyphenate, Jared Nicholas Demarco McPhoy. I was born at the McKenzie Hospital in Linden, Guyana. My parents, Gianna McPhoy and Kenneth Miller were in an on-again, off-again relationship, as my father was married at this point. So yes, you guessed it — I was born out of wedlock...or whatever that shit means. I refuse to say I am a bastard because upon Googling that word I have realised that I am not despicable or unpleasant. Neither am I impure. I am a Museum of Art.

I remember my early days growing up in the Guyanese village of Parika with my mom and grandmother. My grandmother, Millicent McPhoy *(God bless the dead),* was affectionately called 'British Goods,' because she was the hottest girl in town. The men could not take their eyes off of her. I do not remember much of my grandmother from those days, except that I was her 'Fat Boy.' After my mom moved us to the village of Vryheid's Lust, I remember Grandma visiting us and bringing games for me. Like, this one time she brought me a Math game to help me with counting. I can't remember its name but I knew it was a gift of love. Even as I reminisce and recount these events, tears come to my eyes, as I remember Grandma fondly.

Anyways, let me get back on track. What I remember about living in Vryheid's Lust in my early childhood, is poverty. My father didn't give two squats about my mom, and consequently, his children suffered. My mother made three children for him: Briana, Jomelle and myself. I am glad that we don't have his name. I have an older sibling, Renola that my mom made for another man called 'Waps'. My father made two children, Shenika and Shakille, with his wife, Debra. Obviously, they would carry his name, because why not?

My mother was unemployed at the time, so she didn't really have money unless someone gave it to her. I can't say that we were hungry because she made sure we had food to eat. However, I do remember other unfortunate experiences of that time. They are forever etched in my mind. At one point, our electricity was cut off for about six months. I was in grade three at that point, and I remember studying with a candle and having candle wax spots all over my book. Then there was a time when my mom made stewed beef, and guess what? A water frog jumped in the pot so Mom threw the entire stew out. She wouldn't give her children anything that she wouldn't eat herself. Something about living through that time forged a profound sense of determination and resilience within me.

Life changed for the better when my mom got a housekeeping job with Mr. Marcelle Walden. This individual played an instrumental financial role in my story. As a result of this job, she began earning consistently, and was thus able to pay for food, clothing and bills on time. When she first got the job it was near month end, so she only got a week's salary. She confided in my siblings and I that she felt so discouraged and underappreciated in that moment that she had resolved in her heart to quit, until she saw our happy faces as we ate. Tears came to her eyes, she said, as she watched us eating merrily. She changed her mind then, and decided to keep on working so that we could have more happy moments.

At this point in my life Mom used to grow my hair, but she says people used to mistake me for a girl. This is when my *misgenderification* began. Though I was about five or six years old, I was internalizing everything. I didn't realise it at the time, but even the words people spoke about me were being stored. Soon thereafter, Mom cut off all of my hair.

My schooling was always important to me, as it was my way of feeling visible in the world. My academic journey started at Vryheid's Lust Nursery school. I remember Teacher Shaundell being the first educator who I admired, because of her warmth and compassion. Then I progressed to Vryheid's Lust Primary school. Reminiscing on this leg of my journey, I must highlight Miss Michelle who taught me in grades five and six. She stands out to me even now because of how she challenged us as students. If ever we asked an 'easy' question, she would say, *"You are not a baby so I am not spoon feeding you."* This strategy aided the development of my critical thinking skills.

I remember her son Kevon Williams was in my class, and he was my first academic rival. He always got first and me, second. Understandably, at that age I assumed that his mom helped him cheat by prepping him for the questions to come. I remember there was a term when he beat me by a point five, which was then rounded up to one. I was pissed, but this type of competition placed a determination in me that I still carry to this day. It has led to me achieving so much at a young age, like now being an author! So, I may not win but I always win.

While I am still on the topic of primary school, let's talk about my two most embarrassing moments of that period. One bright Monday morning in general assembly, *(I was in either grade five or six, I can't remember which)*, Miss Anita my grade one teacher, marched into the room and commented about persons speaking loudly. Some smart mouth child *(I wish I knew who it was)*, retorted under their breath, *"You don't hear properly."*

I guess she was ready for me that blessed morning because she looked right at me and shouted, *"GO AND STAND ON*

THE STAGE!" Shocked and nervous, I responded honestly that it wasn't me who had made the retort. That only made matters worse as she repeated her order in a harsher and more aggressive tone that I can still hear today.

In embarrassment, I went on the stage and bowed my head for the duration of the assembly. I was the last to leave the room that morning, as is customary for bad behaving students who are sent on the stage. When I went into my classroom afterwards, insult was added to injury as my class teacher, assuming I was guilty, greeted me with, *"Your mouth gon' get you in trouble."*

Well, my dislike for her started right there because how dare she question my innocence? How dare she not defend my honor as her student?

The other embarrassing primary school experience, was the day I went home for lunch and took my school bag with me. I was so absent-minded that I left home and headed back to school without the bag. Upon arriving for my afternoon classes, I *discovered* that my bag was not in my seat. Unaware of my error, I started asking around but everyone replied that they had neither seen nor moved my bag.

I became hysterical, and took my concern to my teacher, who then forsook our afternoon lesson and declared a school search. Some of my classmates searched beneath the school to see if my bag had been dumped there, while another classmate made up a lie about someone dumping my bag in the trench in front of my school. The school called my mom, and she then called my father *(I don't even know why)*. It was a thorough search indeed! But, we came up empty.

I went home after school was dismissed, to find my bag right in my room. I WAS FLABBERGASTED. I know what you are thinking but I promise, I really forgot it was there. To my disdain, Mom made me attend school the next day, which was a Friday. I remember vividly taking small, dramatic steps while I walked to school that morning, trying to somehow delay my inevitable arrival. *On the upside, it was a general assembly day, so there would be opportunity to hide*, or so I thought. If the earth could have opened up and received me on that journey, I would have been a very willing recipient because my heart couldn't handle the embarrassment I knew awaited me.

But! Like everything else in life, I braved the storm and entered the school compound, previously-missing-allegedly-stolen bag in hand. At the general assembly, the Deputy Head Teacher spoke at length about the incident without calling my name. That did not help because most persons already knew it was me. Once again, I hung my head in shame. As I write this, I have a clear understanding of how I developed that toxic habit of bowing my head as I move through life, as if I have anything to be ashamed of.

I am a person who is flawed, but I am also greatly blessed and successful. The thing is this: when you don't know who you are, you will accept the world's definition of you. Most times that definition is inaccurate or incomplete because people project their negative shit on you. The same teacher who had embarrassed me before, was there laughing at my dilemma as I stood in the assembly with my bag. I learned through my experiences, that many educators take their spite and anger out on students when things are not going right in their life. PLEASE STOP THAT SHIT NOW. Because like Miss Adele, you may well end up being spoken of negatively in someone's book.

In hindsight, these moments weren't all bad because I can now look back at them and see growth in myself. After sitting the National Grade Six assessment (a high-stake exam in Guyana) in 2010, I gained a place at President's College *(Wooo-hooo, purple blood all the way!).* This is one of the few Senior Secondary schools in the country.

Let's not even mention the tears I shed when I found out I was accepted at that school. Nope, they were not tears of joy but of great disappointment and sadness, because I thought I could have done better. Was I too hard on myself? Maybe, but like all things in my life God has the final say. I was in for a ride the next five years.

In the upcoming chapters, I will dive deeper into my experience at PC, as we call it for short. I completed my secondary education in 2015 with two grade one's, seven grade two's and one grade three *(in the blessed Mathematics)*. I successfully gained entry into Guyana's premier teaching training institutions, formally known as the Cyril Potter College of Education (CPCE). The two years I spent here were really something else. It turns out I did not know myself despite what I thought. I made friends with the right people, but that too turned out unexpectedly. *(More on this in another chapter).*

After finishing CPCE in 2017, I started my teaching career at Annandale Secondary School where I still am attached. I enrolled at the University of Guyana in 2018, which was record-breaking considering that most teachers have to wait at least two years to study at the university level. This is because the school system (at that time), operated on a seniority basis, meaning whoever started teaching first gets to go the University if they are desirous.

Annandale had four teachers completing their Bachelor's degree at the time that I joined the staff, so those spaces opened up in the following year. I am laughing here as I remember one of my former colleagues (who took a transfer from Annandale) saying to me, *"You gon' gah wait long fuh duh."* In my mind I replied, *"You must not know 'bout me,"* in my best Beyoncé voice, because I was set on attending UG that year.

One blessing about Annandale Secondary, is that most teachers had already attended UG, so the ones who had not, were likely uninterested. This was good for me. I started UG in 2018 and completed it IN A PANDEMIC *(Elsa's voice)!* This was clearly a very unique situation, because the university was forced to adapt to the new forced way of teaching. Interestingly, the period of studying online made me realize how much I hate doing in person exams and presentations.

Online presented me with the same opportunity to excel without the anxiety. I was gaining bare A's (with the exception of a Reading course where I missed the A by TWO marks). *Miss, if you're reading this, I am still pissed with you but, whatever.* For much of the program I was in the 2.8 range. I am proud to say I graduated in March of 2021 with a credit, GPA 3.1. God really used this tough situation to bring light and blessing.

This reminds me of that story in the Bible where God used a cloud to give light to the children of Israel, inadvertently giving darkness to the enemy so they could not catch God's people. During what was a difficult time for most, I have seen the divine goodness of God. My heart overflows with gratitude for what He has done for my family and me. My story is a unique one, but one that I know many persons will be able to relate to. I suggest that you sit back, grab something nice to eat and enjoy this reading of my life. Please be warned of my very subtle humor. Don't go choking on your food and blaming me for it now! Be inspired to inspire as we explore a life through God's grace!

CHAPTER TWO:

Coming Out

You've read the title at least twice now. I know some of you are either very shocked, or bracing yourself as you wonder if I'll finally come out and say that I am gay. Truth is, when it comes to my sexuality, I have always been conflicted but never not confused. It was merely a battle of what I was taught I *should* feel, versus what I *do* feel. In my experience, one of the hardest things to do is ignore a feeling, especially one that either comes naturally or comes as a result of the hand you were dealt.

I have childhood memories of my father visiting my mom often, and they would be in their bedroom doing God-knows-what. I had no idea what sex was at that point, but what I knew was that every time they were finished doing God-knows-what, my mother would give him my towel to use. I used to be so annoyed about that. This inflicted a trauma upon me resulting in the hatred I was now developing for my mom.

I remember one day they called my sister Brianna and I into their room, and we watched them kiss passionately. You are probably asking yourself what kind of parents would do that

to their children. I can't answer because I don't know either.
I remember wanting them to stop but at that moment the right words eluded me. I remember my sister turning to me with a confused expression. Eventually, we both found the words to cry, *"STOP!"* but they didn't. Next thing I know, we were outside the room and I could distinctly hear my mother's moans.

This marked the beginning of an unhealthy relationship with my sexuality. I was unaware of the impact that moment had on me then. I have hated my father for so many years. I bore so much resentment for him and the fact that my mother tried to force me to have a relationship with him, caused me to resent her too.

I remember when I was in secondary school, I used to teach at the Sunday school in Better Hope, along with the pastor's daughter. I felt, with good reason, like she was not as committed as I was. Though we lived close to each other, I often traveled alone in the hot sun to teach.

I always hated walking to the church alone. There was a shed (now a wash bay) on the route, where people would lime and wait for buses. The guys who loitered here always hurled negative comments about my body and sexuality. On one occasion, a guy turned said to his two friends as I was walking by, *"Watch duh back."*

The other guy chimed in and said, *"One of them town man gon geh fuh go in that,"* to which Guy Number Three responded, *"I know I want to go in duh."* I felt so naked, vulnerable and embarrassed. They had the audacity to call me gay, when they were the ones talking gay about me *(oh, the hypocrisy)*.

After that day, I really dreaded passing that area. After a while I told the pastor that my time at the Sunday school was coming to an end, and that his daughter would have to carry the ministry. Another memorable incident happened at church. One day I was entering the church, when Gavin groped my man boobs, before he and his friend James burst out laughing. Again, that now familiar feeling of shame and disgrace overtook me. I never told my mom or anyone about that incident. It was just another that caused me to keep bowing my head as I moved through my village.

I was inadvertently fueling their hate speech towards me because I didn't stand up for myself. Looking back, I sometimes I wonder why I didn't put them in their place from day one. But come to think of it, I didn't know I was me *(in my best TD Jakes voice)*, so in those days I let their words reign victoriously over me. In secondary school every time I passed a group of boys, I was referred to as "Lula."

Let me give you the back story of how that name came about. I was in form two, and Sherese *(my crush)*, and I were in a bus with some dumb fools from her batch. They were one year younger than I was. The bus broke down and the driver went out to examine and fix the issue. The driver was taking so long that I grew impatient and was about to leave the bus, when the doors shut and Akeem, the Dumb Fools' ring leader, started talking shit about me. He taunted that I was going to be buggered by the driver and that I would bawl out, *"Lula!"*

What was most embarrassing, was that my so-called friend and crush Sherese, was laughing me. She didn't bother defending my honor. I was so full of shame that afternoon as I sat back down in the bus. I never said a word. Every single time those boys saw me on the road or at school they would shout, *"Lula!"* and I would ignore them. That was the way I dealt with stuff that bothered me — I pretended that they didn't exist, because if they don't exist, I don't have to face them.

The word "fire" was thrown at me in a derogatory manner, indicating that I was different from everybody else and needed to be cleansed of my impurities. (Or at least that's how I interpreted it). The Dumb Fools made my life a living hell. Thank God for the other members of the famous four crew: Eric, Marina and Sheena, who made the ending of secondary school worthwhile.

In my community many of the guys who didn't know me personally referred to me as *'that aunty man one.'* This broke me even further. I remember walking on the road and a guy turned to his friend and said of me, *"He is an aunty man you know,"* and both of them started laughing.

Did he intentionally say it for me to hear? It would appear so. The irony of all of this is that I was never given a chance to individuate. People quickly decided who I was, and the sad part is I gave them permission and opportunity to. Not once did I ever stand up for myself, because I felt so vulnerable and helpless around those terrible people.

At school whenever I saw the Dumb Fools or the bigger students in the technical stream, I would quickly change route because I was tired of their taunts. Sometimes it was impossible to change route because they already clocked me coming on the catwalk. (That is what we called it at PC. The catwalk was like a corridor that you had to traverse in order to gain access to certain classrooms and buildings).

I remember one time I shared a collage on Facebook that I created with a friend. Low and behold Akeem commented, *"You are doing well for an Aunty Man lol I'm joking."* I deleted his comment and the picture right away. I knew that if my mom had seen his comment, she would have gotten into it with him right under the post, intending to help me. One thing about my mom: she defended me in everything.

She did this even though I know she often didn't understand how and why I behaved in the manner that I did.

In form two, I was obsessed with a game on Facebook called Coco Girls. My mom disapproved of me playing that game because in her opinion, it was for girls. The game was basically about your avatar playing games to gain points that could be used to purchase and wear high fashion clothing. I didn't see anything wrong with the game so I went ahead and played it despite Mom's disapproval, but I was sure to not share it on Facebook.

This one time I did and Kesha Carel from 2R commented, *"No offense, but are you gay?"*

My mom saw the comment and responded to Kesha thinking she was doing me a favor but I was embarrassed. This led me to delete my entire Coco Girls photo album on Facebook. Later on, I stopped playing the game all together, because my mom started to police me whenever I played it, to ensure that I didn't share any more photos.

I have always seen the world differently from most — through a non-gender lens. As I grew older, and especially through my studies of Women and Literature, I came to realise that society perpetuates gender stereotypes that binaries are expected to uphold. So what if I like things that most boys didn't? That doesn't make me gay or obscene.

I already felt like an outcast. I felt unloved. I felt unwanted. So, I started rebelling in subtle ways to my mom and different figures of authority. I used sarcasm as a defense mechanism, and to this day I sometimes retreat to my briefcase of smart wit to let people know that I am not the one or the two, to play with. I have always been intelligent so most persons looked past my 'girlish' behavior and focused on my intellect. I used that to my advantage.

'Shade Boss' is what I was called, because of my skillful use of the verbal assault. I just knew — and still do to this day — know how to get on people's nerve and under their skin. As a result of my observant nature, I am able to assess people and attack their weakness or insecurity. That was my way of feeling victorious over the many verbal attacks that came my way. Throwing shade just came naturally to me.

I remember one Sunday when Sis Rolice, (dancer, worship leader and youth leader) exceeded her time limit with the dancers. As a result, I was not able to host children ministry that afternoon. So, guess what I did? I wrote a lovely status message on Facebook saying that karma comes for those who deserve it. As if expecting me to shade her, she responded to my status with, *"Lol is who you throwing shade at?"* I quickly deleted the post, because I had gotten her attention which was all I wanted. Next time she would know better than to go over her time.

I can recall another occasion when I used my words as weapons. I was between the ages of 15 and 17, chilling at home with my siblings. I responded to something one of them said.

Annoyed, my mom turned to me and asked, *"is everything you gah respond to?"*

To which I retorted sharper than ever, *"it's clap back season."*

To that my mom responded, *"Are you gay?"*

Now try to imagine hearing this question coming from your mother. Suffice it to say my resentment for her grew all the more. I started withdrawing from my family members because I always felt like the odd one out, the outcast, the misfit.

So, if you ask me now whether I am gay, my answer is YES! A THOUSAND TIMES YES! I have learnt a long time ago that *gay* means *happy* and I am one of the happiest persons you'll ever meet. That's because I have endured my darkness and I am not going back to that place.

I remember contemplating suicide and running away from home. I just couldn't take the pressure that I felt was on me, to conform to what everyone else sees. I have since found my light and I choose to stand boldly and unapologetically in it. I reclaim that word 'Gay' as my own, because many persons behave as if that word is a curse. We have allowed society to use that word in discriminatory ways to ostracize people and make them feel 'othered'.

To be Gay is to be happy, and being happy is a state of mind. My joy is fueled from the inside of my spirit and soul not from external circumstances and people. I choose to be a light in this world of darkness, because we never know what people may be going through. Do not underestimate the power of a compliment and kindness. Let's strive towards leaving a pleasant taste in someone's mouth. When people think about you they should smile because their encounter was one filled with positivity.

I am currently living my Best Black Gay life to my fullest potential, and YOU SHOULD TOO!

CHAPTER THREE:

The Misgenderification of Jared and The Evolution of My Alter Ego "Jasmine"

I have always felt misgendered. Many people thought that I was too feminine because of how I spoke, walked and carried myself. This in turn caused me to always feel safer in the presence of women. Their company became my safe place. I felt like I could connect with them more than I could with any man. My interest in them was never sexual but platonic, one of great admiration. Because my first example of leadership came from a woman (my mom), I always felt threatened by male authority figures. It was 'the battle of the egos,' as I like to call it. I would look for my mom in every female teacher, seeking out that familiar sense of comfort and acceptance.

Why are you behaving like a girl?

Stop it with your girlish antics!

You are too much!

I internalized these statements from others and played them over and over in my mind. Eventually, I began to contemplate the fact that maybe God made a mistake with me. *Maybe I am supposed to be a girl, because nothing about me is manly outside of the penis that I have.* This kind of thinking led to the creation of "Jasmine", my feminine alter ego.

Jasmine got to do all the things I wish I could have as Jared. She would dress sexy but decent, and get all the guys that Jared was crushing on. Let's not talk about the sex! She was getting it in because as Jared I could do none of those things. I remember one time I traveled to Linden for vacation, to stay with relatives.

My cousin Jason, in introducing me to his friend said, *"This is my cousin Jared. He is here on vacation for me to teach him how to be a man."*

I didn't even know how to respond, but I was so used to this kind of comment that I just let it be. But Jason went on to prompt me to speak.

"Say something," he said.

The moment I spoke I regretted it because Jason commented, *"You see how girlish he sounds."*

People have always tried to fix me as if something was wrong with me to begin with. I let them try, because I really didn't know who I was. When you don't know your worth, people will walk all over you, dragging you for filth. In the presence of men, I would perform as masculine, to hopefully avoid criticism. I used the word "perform" because it felt like an act to me. I was so uncomfortable. My best times were when I was in the presence of my female friends, who I could emotionally connect to.

I was happiest as Jasmine. As Jasmine, I could create the life I thought I deserved — one of happiness and true contentment. I remember playing around with makeup and specifically, putting on eyeshadow. My mom, unaware, sent me on an errand to collect something from her friend, Miss Trinity. Upon my arrival, Miss Trinity noticed the eyeshadow and immediately called my mom. So, when I got home my mom called me to inspect my eyes and said, *"Are you wearing makeup?"* I denied it but there was no point. She went for the belt and put a sound thrashing on me.

Did I regret my actions in that moment? Certainly! But in hindsight, I had every right to be curious because I was a child just exploring life. I still tried on makeup afterwards though. I remember being closeted in the bath room and fiddling with my older sister's make up kit, especially her bold red lipstick. I enjoyed kissing a square of toilet paper and admiring the lip print, because come on, I do have great lips.

When I was around age eight, my younger sister Brianna and I would play dolly house, in which we would pretend to be housewives running the home while our husbands were at work. One day, Mom called me inside the house and whispered to me that men who are in relationship with other men are called gays, and that if I ever spoke of having a husband again, she would beat me. I was forced to replace "husband" with "wife" in my future dolly house games, but it felt so wrong to me at the time.

I used to try on my cousin, Lavern's stockings when she wasn't at home, and I used to shave my legs because I noticed that women did that. In my little world, humans didn't have to perform specific gender roles — they just lived. I was modeling the behavior of those who I admired in my life — women — but all I felt from them was rejection. I did not quite understand why they rejected me. I revered them but they despised me. I guess from their point of view, I was turning into someone society would taunt and hate, so they sought to toughen me up before the world did.

Though I did so well in primary school, I was not focused on my academics between grade seven and fourth form. I have literally entered exam rooms not knowing ONE THING and exiting knowing I had failed. When it was time for preparation for CSEC examinations in 2015, my mother could not afford the lessons. My father had promised to pay the fee but never did.

In fourth form I started doing English A and B lessons at Miss Fernand. She was not my favorite because I held a grudge against her from second form when she embarrassed me by mimicking how I would suck my finger and walk with my butt pushed out. What kind of adult makes fun of a child? I guess I didn't have my luck with some teachers, eh? The lesson fees were piling up. I stopped attending because every time Miss Fernand saw me she would ask about her money.

Sure, this was her right but where was the compassion and understanding for a child who just couldn't afford it? Was I supposed to go steal or have sex for the money? Mind you, it was about 4000 Guyanese dollars (approximately USD$20) that we owed. The straw that broke the camel's back was when Miss Fernand called me into the staff room where her desk was. Her confederate, my English teacher was right there at the desk next to her.

She turned to me and asked, *"Where is my money?"*

I responded, *"My mom doesn't have it as yet."*

She audaciously replied, *"Tell your mother to go and get a job. Other people do it. Because I need my money!"*

Even as I write this, I feel a gush of emotions flowing through my veins. If I was one to curse I would say, *"F U*

Miss! You were a bully and I know that Karma is on the horizon."

I remember relaying this information to my mom word for word and she was so angry and sad that I had to endure those cruel words. Mom quickly gathered up the money and came to school to meet with her. Would you believe Miss Fernand changed the story, claiming she never said those things? I didn't expect more from her as I said she was a full-blown hypocrite. The last thing I will say about her is that when I finished secondary school and started CPCE she would always ask me, *"You still at college?"* as if I was expected to drop out but the joke's on her.

Look at me now — established with my first degree and writing my debut book about my life. LOOK AT GOD, HE HAS DONE IT AGAIN, SHOWING UP AND OUT FOR ME. He can for you too, so don't be bitter. Let Go and Let God. As hard as life may be at times, He knows BEST and will only allow the BEST to come out of a situation if you let Him.

Oh, but I toughened up! I recall another unfortunate experience, this one involving social media. When I was in form five, I uploaded a picture of myself to Facebook with the caption "#Misfit." Truth is, #Misfit was a trendy expression among young Christians at the time, who believed they are called to stand out instead of conforming to the world's standard.

My mom did not care about that context and demanded that I changed the caption. Her reason was that people already thought I was gay, and the caption would give them more to talk about. Her problem was that the first three letters (MIS), appeared feminine. Even now I can hear her suggesting that I put "#MrFit" instead. Again, I was in a situation where it felt like she was not on my side. Yet, I can acknowledge that her intention was to protect me.

As I told you earlier, my mom allowed my hair to grow out until about age six. I had edges, roots and of course, baby hair before any of those things were trendy. She told me that people often commented that her daughter, (referring to me), was pretty. She would have to correct them and assert that I am a boy, not a girl. Eventually, Mom cut off all my hair.

I have no recollection of these events, but I have seen pictures of myself as a child and if I do say so myself, I have always been top tier. It's like people say: God was in His Birkin when He made me. I believe that although I didn't understand what was happening to me, I internalized those words and accepted them as truth.

I used to think that women had it easier than men, until I was exposed to the study of feminism through Women and Literature. *(Shout out to one of the BEST lecturers at UG Mrs. APC)*. I came to understand how much society, especially men, hated women and I found that to be so weird.

Every day women lose more and more of their autonomy over their bodies, because of legislation and religious biases. Women are deemed to be "the second sex," as Simone De Beauvoir writes, (or as I like to say — the invisible sex). The question I always ask is how can the group that forms the majority of the world's population be seen as anything but excellent?

I want to take this time to applaud the works of all feminists, past and present. I thank you for the fight towards women's equality because as you must realise by now, I am a feminist. Many men love to objectify women and use them as commodities to satisfy their sexual pleasures. I remember when a cousin of mine who used to live with us, got his girlfriend pregnant. When they went to do the ultrasound, it was discovered that the fetus is female.

When they returned home that afternoon, I noticed the sadness and anger in my cousin's face. The young mother-to-be silently held in her joy, in an attempt to pacify him. Being inquisitive, I asked the fetus's sex and my cousin responded reluctantly, *"A girl."* Referring to the future mother of his daughter he said, *"She lucky that belly gone too far fuh get throw away."*

These words are etched in my memory, because I was shocked that one could hate his child before they were even born. In many cases, women's lives are determined for them even before they leave the womb. Years after this incident with my cousin, one of my friends got pregnant.

When I asked her the gender of the child, she said excitedly, *"It's a girl!"*

But I noticed a familiar hesitation before she answered that reminded me too much of my cousin's behavior.

Thus, I asked a follow-up question, *"What did your husband say?"*

She took a breath before disclosing that he was pissed, and blamed her for the baby being female. I was flabbergasted. Audacity must be for sale on the black market, because people are wilding out these days. Is it COVID-19 that has them acting a fool or something in the water? I really do not know.

She went on to say that she cried for days after her husband's comment, until she shared her frustrations with the doctor who educated her. The doctor let her know that it is her husband's sperm that determines the gender of the baby, so if anything, he is the reason why the baby is a girl.

Men: y'all big and have sense. Stop doing this nonsense to our women. It's time to start respecting women for their greatness and acknowledging their value. It appears most guys specifically want a soccer team of boys. What would happen if this world was filled with only men? Think about it and come back to me with the answer. I for one cannot imagine this world without the queens that we get to coexist with.

My alter ego, Jasmine was created as a form of release. She provided me with a comfortable, safe space t o express my femininity. One of the problems with our society is that it does not encourage or allow us to express both sides of ourselves, that is, our masculine and feminine sides.

Both of these are locked into our biological makeup. I do believe that when we ignore or suppress one side of our being, we create an imbalance that results in what I call 'gender extremes.' This can lead to toxic masculinity or toxic femininity, where persons are extreme in their efforts to avoid being identified as the opposite sex.

I tried to mask my softer side with my intellect, by causing a distraction with my big and bright personality. I remember when I started working how I would create these scenarios of myself as Jasmine: the clothes, hair, nails and shoes I would wear for work. At one point she/ I even had a family, we were married.

Over time as I began to step more into myself as Jared Nicholas Demarco McPhoy, I begin to see that I have value as a man, that I was created on purpose, for purpose. Therefore, I have no reason to dim the bright light that God has put within me.

Jasmine began to slowly die because I realised that I don't and shouldn't need an alter ego to live and experience life fully. The thing is I am human (which is a truth that I resented for a long time because I felt it poked at my limitations. Only God is perfect. I have decided that I will accept and learn from my mistakes because they only make me better.

I would be a dirty liar if I told you all that I am 100% confident in my sexuality. #HELLNO. I still have my triggers and sometimes I even think about transitioning. But when those feelings come up, I always ask myself *where is this stemming from and how can I use it to build me up.*

So, to YOU reading this book right now, in case you have never heard it before: YOU ARE MORE THAN ENOUGH!
Know that it's okay to be unsure of know who you are, and how to express your sexuality healthily. One day it will always make sense and when it does, I encourage you to live your truth boldly.

I love you and I am rooting for you. You got this champ!

CHAPTER FOUR:

My Sexual Awakening

I remember the first time I played with my penis to the point where I climaxed and a clear, sticky substance came out #GraphicMuch! A guy in my class named Romel, would always boast about the fact that he masturbates. He was so proud of that. Through him, I got to understand what masturbation was and I became curious to try it out myself. After that first ejaculation, I longed for that feeling again and so the habit of masturbation began.

One time I was caught doing it in the bathroom at home. My mom came in and I denied it to the gods, but deep down I know I was guilty. Although what I was engaged in was natural for any teen boy, I felt ashamed of this newfound joy in my life. I remember rubbing my penis on the bedpost because of how it made me feel. Ejaculation became different for me because I started producing sperm and the colour of it changed from the first time.

My cousin Shamal, who used to live with us at the time, had a lot of porn on his phone, so I started stealing his phone to engage in watching pornography, this was my first encounter with it. I loved it because it gave me an erection and when I played with myself, I ejaculated. It was so euphoric for me.

These habits got so out of hand that I was almost caught.

My cousin said to my mom, *"Juhred took my phone to watch blues."* I denied that shit to the gods!

Over time these newfound joys of watching pornography and masturbating birthed another curiosity within me to watch gay porn. At first, it was weird but after I discovered what my favorite kind was, there was no going back. I am a very sensual person so porn that felt rough and painful was not my scene. I enjoyed the ones where there were lots of kissing, rubbing and sucking.

Watching gay porn widened my vocabulary in the area of homosexuality. I learned the meaning of words like *tops*, *bottoms* and *verse*. Watching gay porn then led me to start imagining myself having sex with different guys.

My lust for men increased to the point where I could masturbate to the mental image of me and them having sex. I have a very wild imagination, so the sensations always felt so real. I must reiterate I have never had sex, nor even kissed anyone on the lips.

Except if we count the fake kiss from Lew *(a close female friend turned stranger.)* Don't worry, she has her very own chapter coming up. God knows why none of the men I had a crush on ever made a move on me. I don't know where I would be, had I engaged in those sexual acts in real life.

I'll confide in you about a time when a guy tried hitting on me. It was a guy who worked an internet café, who I must say is very DL (short for *down low* aka *undercover gay)*. I went to the establishment to get my work printed. I got his number from my friend and decided to send him my work, so that it would be ready for payment and pickup when I arrived. This was a typical modus operandi for those who wanted quick services. What he saw, was an opportunity for something else...which I had a feeling he would.

When I arrived, he said, *"Sir, sorry about that. I forgot about you. Let me print your work out now."*

While I was waiting for him to print the work, I noticed in my peripherals that he was texting and looking over at me, but I avoided any eye contact with him. I received my prints, thanked him and left. When my phone connected to the Wi-Fi at home later that evening, I saw a message from him.

The message said, *"You have such wonderful lips. I just want to kiss them."*

I wanted to vomit in my mouth. I felt ashamed as if I was doing a bad thing. I only confided this information to one of my good friends and a colleague at the time who was very overly spiritual. The truth is, he was not my type. If he was my type or had money, I might have accepted his offer, and deep down this is why I felt so ashamed. I wonder if that's how other guys I liked viewed me. Talk about unrequited love.

I have always found that when I am surrounded by guys, I bring out their softer side. I am not sure if that was their way of connecting with me. This was a side of me that I never really shared with anyone because let's face it: Guyana is very conservative in its views, and people who identify with the LGBTQIA community are ostracized point blank.

MY ADDICTION TO PORNOGRAPHY AND MASTURBATION:
(Don't Hold My Hands)

Allow me to paraphrase something Andra Day said in an interview that really caught my attention. She said that we all are addicted to something, it's just that our addiction manifests itself differently. That resonated so much with me, because of my attraction to men and addiction to pornography and masturbation. All these things made me feel sick and less than others.

As much as I tried to purge myself from these things, for some reason I just could not. It felt as if I would be cutting out part of who I was, which would leave me feeling deformed and disabled. I realised I was addicted to these behaviors when I simply could not stop engaging in them.

They had such a hold over me, that simple things would ignite a strange fire within me and lead me to these acts. They were like my cocaine or heroin. After a while, I tried to stop judging people who I noticed are addicted to these substances, because I grew to understand what it was to be addicted. Let's face it: addiction is sweet but the consequences sting badly, leaving a permanent mark.

TO ANYONE GOING THROUGH AN ADDICTION, I SEE YOU AND I LOVE YOU.

WITH ENOUGH HARD WORK AND DETERMINATION,

YOU CAN GET THROUGH THIS STRONGER THAN YOU WERE BEFORE.

I used to judge people harshly for being addicted to sex, smoking, drinking or other things, until I came to realise that I only hated those people because they reminded me of my own addictions, and my brokeness. After ejaculating, the porn you are watching doesn't make you feel that tingle any more. You just feel sick. Then the guilt starts creeping in. The guilt of what would my mom, or anyone who knows me think of me and my faith in God if they knew about this hidden sin?

This addiction led me to do some things that I am not proud of like masturbating twice in the church washroom. The first time my home was crowded and I needed that release badly. I loaded the desired porn video on my phone so it would play outside of the Wi-Fi zone. I opened up the church (because I used to keep the key), and I went straight into the washroom and engaged in the act.

Of course, I felt some guilt at the moment but the thing with addiction is that it is a monster that you yield your power to. Addiction abuses your dignity and leaves you with nothing if it is not stopped in time. Afterward, I cleaned up myself and the environment, locked up the church, and went back home as if nothing had happened.

The second time I did this was years later. I was so horny that I rushed into the church washroom. This time the church had Wi-Fi so I was able to go on Twitter *(yes, Twitter has a very dark side. Big ups to the #TwitterAfterDark crew)*. I found my favorite page and went to town on myself. Afterward, I had that familiar guilt-ridden feeling of how did I get here? Why am I doing this? I need help!

The thing with addiction is that it takes so much time from you. I often would wonder about what I could have done with all the time I spent watching porn. Through watching porn, I came to realise that I desired to have sex with men more than ever.

How could I ever come to tell people these things about me? I felt like I was going mad. It is so crazy, that for many days I felt like I was living without oxygen. I turned to academic fulfillment but that still wasn't enough. I remember completing my Bachelor's in Education-English in 2020 *(Big up to the pandemic crew and all the COVID graduates. We did it!)*. I felt so empty. The success of this venture didn't feel the way I had envisioned it. After taking some time to reflect, I came to the realization that I had attached my feeling of accomplishment to external validation.

I did not quit on the triggers because I was too weak to do so. Also, pornography and masturbation were where I felt truly like myself. I loved watching shows with explicit sexual content that fueled this strange fire burning within me.

Another major thing about me that I should mention at this point, is that I have never been in a relationship with anyone before. This is because everyone I liked never liked me back, and I did not like the small number of people who I discovered had a crush on me. Plus, as I was diving deeper into exploring my sexual identity, I knew that I wasn't craving intimacy with women at all, so why waste their time?

At the same time, I was so scared of gay sex. What if I shit myself while in the act? What if I am recorded in the act? What if the guy pranks me, and I become a viral sensation? Because as we know, a porn video can and will go viral before anything positive does.

Every time someone asked me if I had a girlfriend, I would feel so awkward because in my mind I'm like can't they read the room? One time someone asked me if I had a boyfriend and I laughed, but I was shocked at their bravery. Every time people brought up the topic of homosexuality, I would become very quiet because this plucked at a nerve deep within me.

Andra Day in her song "Gin and Juice" says, *"Don't hold my hands / let go my hands."* I have always felt like my addictions were people holding on to me tightly. It's like my addiction says to me, *"you birthed me and nurtured me and now you want to let me go? Never."* It's like it says to me, *"you letting me go is killing me and I'm not going to let you do that to me."*

To the person reading this: I want you to know that you can and will overcome any addictions that have you bound. Be patient and gentle with yourself in the process. I'm sending peace and love your way.

CHAPTER FIVE:

Friends: How Many Of Us Have Them?

I have always been big on friendships because at one point in my life I felt greatly rejected by the people in my home. I felt like the unlovable sibling. I am probably being dramatic about this but it's who I am. The first person who I considered to be my Friend was a guy named Tevin Marks. All I remember was the fact that we talked a lot, and had fun. That was enough for me in a friendship at this stage.

I do remember one conflict we had in Grade 5 where our class teacher said that I was not going to get second but that Tevin would, which really pissed me off. This created a slight rift between us until I proved myself and got second, keeping him in his rightful third position *(lol shady, I know)*. Tevin's father was also very kind to me, giving me money whenever he saw me. I was very happy about this because in those days I used to take $20 to school because that's all mom could afford.

Poverty is not a joke. If you are reading this and you are in poverty, I want you to promise me and yourself that you are going to work very hard to become the change in your family to break this vicious cycle. Trust me, you won't regret it.

Now back to my friendships. After graduating from primary school, Tevin and I drifted apart as we did not pass to go to the same high school. His mother sent for him to come and live in the United States with her. I just accepted the reality that our friendship would fizzle out because what could I do about it?

Marina Hawkins was the first friend I made in secondary school. How could I forget? She came up to me while I was under the catwalk and introduced herself. What I remember most about her from that day, was that she had a very cute lunch kit in her hand and a haversack on her back. I was so happy to meet her because she was very kind and sweet. Unfortunately, our friendship didn't take off until we were in third form.

Marina had caught Julianna Locke and Julianna's boyfriend in a compromising position behind the school's washroom, and she reported it. People were judging her for reporting what she saw. Being my inquisitive self, I wanted to know every detail. The girls I used to hang around at that time (Christa, Elisa and Jayanna) were not so fond of Marina.

They thought that she acted a bit 'holier than thou.' I liked her because she was the kind of Christian I aspired to be. I remember regularly telling people nasty things (for example that their mother's private part is roaming and foaming), and listening to worldly music! In those days, I didn't know how to fit in as a Christian, because let's be real — being a Christian is not trendy in secondary school.

In that same year, I connected with Eric and Sheena who were in the class 3Q. They weren't best of friends but I remember causing a big cuss out between them. I was the go between and let's just say the cussing was grand. Many didn't like me because of what I did but I could have cared less because I already was not their favorite.

After this incident, I was scared because Eric told me that Sheena had an Uncle who worked obeah, so I feared supernatural retaliation. My fear was that she was going to work obeah on me using one of my pictures on Facebook. I vividly remember that I was so afraid that I would check my skin for marks or rotting because that's what I thought the obeah would do. Don't judge me — the obeah I saw on African Moods was hella scary.

In fourth form Eric, Marina, Sheena and I formed our own group. We had many names for our group: Famous 4, Studious 4 and JEMS (the name of our group chat to this DAY). The three of them helped me to endure secondary school because at one point the taunting from the other students became unbearable.

These three classmates were my guardian angels. We each had our strengths and weaknesses which made us the perfect group. We shared our own secrets along with people's business (which was my favorite part). We had our ups and downs but nothing could separate us.

Eric was the bold one in the group, the great debater and cuss bird. There was one occasion I can recall where a girl named Mesha said his mouth was stink, and he let her have it in true Eric style. Most people assumed that he was gay which caused a rift in our relationship because many people thought I was gay too. Some people believed he and I were together which angered me deeply. Can't two males be platonic? It was just because we were different and not overtly masculine like the others who fit into society's mold.

Marina was still the quiet, gentle soul that I had met years before in form one. In fact, she was a bit of a pushover in the sense that she would allow people to treat her anyway while she remained silent. That was then because if you try that now she would handle you properly. I remember the first time I heard Marina curse. (This was after high school). I was flabbergasted to say the least. Marina really was the calm to the storm for me.

Sheena or "Shik Shik" as we like to call her, had a laugh that was so lawless and intoxicating. Being the funny guy that I am, I loved making her laugh. She was straightforward and bold. After I got over the fear of her working obeah on me, I grew to love her company. Can we talk about how intelligent she is? I figured this out because every time we had an Integrated Science test she would ace them and I was like what!

As you may realise by now, this trio was my rock and my anchor and I am so glad that we have remained friends throughout the years. We continued having ups and downs but what is life without them? Marina, Eric and I are educators, while Sheena is an Immigration Officer and a whole wife and mother. I couldn't be any prouder of my friends.

Honestly, I sometimes wonder if we are still friends because of tradition and habit. But then we meet up and it's like we never left. I am beyond grateful for our bond. I am also grateful that when I am with them, I can truly be myself without fear of judgment or ridicule. When they are around me they are motivated to keep on pushing themselves because I will accept nothing less from them.

When you find great friends, you should hold onto them with everything that you've got. Be bold enough to define the kind of friendships that you want and ensure that each party agrees. As you will read in this next chapter failed expectations can lead to serious heartbreak and disappointment.

After leaving secondary school in June of 2015, I moved on to the Cyril Potter College of Education in September of that year. I had no friends joining the institution with me so I was lonely and alone. I missed my JEMS crew very much. Marina and Eric had chosen to pursue their studies at CAPE (Caribbean Advanced Proficiency Examination), while Sheena went on to study Sociology at the University of Guyana so we were all ambitious and thriving. Even though I was happy for them, I really wished we were all together at CPCE because truth be told, we would have been a force to be reckoned with.

In 2016 it was time for me to have a Teaching Practice partner as teacher trainees were being sent into schools for observations. I was placed with Miss Rehanna Housley, who I knew from President's College. We were not friends, but cordial. I welcomed the opportunity to get to know her better because she was a very mysterious person and I was curious. Plus, I had no other choice because the practice was compulsory and partner selections were final.

We merely tolerated each other at first. Got our work done and engaged in no discussions of our personal lives. Over time we clashed about the creation of our lesson plans because we both liked our own way. I am happy to say it all worked out in the end.

I had great admiration for her work ethic. She really could have handled any student from the lowest to the highest level and they all respected her. I, on the other hand, approached most situations with insecurities. Full disclosure: this is one of my toxic traits.

I tend to behave as though I didn't earn the right to the spaces that I am afforded the opportunity to be in. I hid under her protection by shadowing her wherever she went — whether it be to the canteen or class — until I was able to gain some semblance of confidence. I remember one day she came into the staff room and her countenance was way off. There and then I detected that something was wrong with her.

I asked, *"What's wrong?"* She went on to tell me about this argument that she had with her mom. We talked through it and I transparently related to her that I was facing something similar, so we bonded over our shared trauma. This blossomed into us chatting on WhatsApp and following each other on the socials.

She was the first friend I ever bought a gift for with my own money. I appreciated our friendship so much that I wanted to express it in that way. In return, she bought me a gift for my birthday and we have never stopped doing that.

We have had our fair share of downs. I have often felt throughout our friendship that when I needed her the most she wasn't there to support me. When I needed a guarantor to sign the contract I had with the Ministry of Education as a result of my release to go to the University of Guyana. Let's just say Rehanna was not there for me in the way I expected her to be.

(Please remember that I always approach situations by being dramatic first and logical second). I pulled away from her because in my mind, she didn't love me. If I was ridiculous and had overreacted I was in good company because others who I told of the situation were equally shocked about her refusal to be my guarantor. Such is life. *"People will be people and God will be God,"* as my dear Reverend Lucy Natasha says.

Despite our disagreements what I love most about us is that we always find time to talk about our feelings and issues. In talking about it we both would do better and move on. We would go out on friend dates to lunch, dinner or the movies. She is more outgoing than I am but there's something about when we link up — it's like this fire between us comes alive. This was our quality time with each other despite the business of our adult lives. We graduated from the University of Guyana together and to this day keep in contact.

I believe that I have attachment issues, as when I like or love someone, I hold onto them tightly and feel threatened by any other person who tries to get close to them. I am that friend who likes to message you every day. Can you imagine my shock when I found out that people didn't want to talk to me every day? I have had to make compromises and to some extent, settle for less because most people just didn't satisfy my demand.

One thing I have learned is that no one friend can be everything to you. You really need different friends for different occasions like food friend, movie friend, confidant friend, gossip friend, adventure friend etc. Some friends are versatile and because thus can overlap in different areas, but they will still have limits. Expecting one friend to be all things to you will inevitably bring you disappointment.

Defining boundaries in friendship is paramount for any healthy relationship to last. Some friends are givers and some are takers, so know your limits. I am a giver especially when it comes to my time. I have gone out of my way to help a friend when I would not have thought to do the same thing for my family.

You see the thing is when I felt rejected and unloved as a child it was friendships that helped me. I just did not feel like I could have expressed my true self to anyone because could they handle this mess? That's how I viewed myself then.

The last friend I want to highlight is like an angel to me: my dear Renicia Hamer. Full disclosure: at one point I genuinely disliked her because she had this "miss biggity" attitude that I couldn't handle. I remember when we wrote the NGSA exam I outperformed her and passed for President's College, while she was placed at Bygeval Secondary but was later transferred to Hope Secondary school. Throughout high school Pastor would boast of her excellent grades which were higher than mine.

When my pastor heard that I was not going to any lessons, and that I needed help with Mathematics, she asked Renicia to help me with the subject. She agreed. In retrospect, I think this was the beginning of our appreciation for each other.

She assisted me faithfully spending her passage coming to my house to ensure that I grasped the main concepts. I passed the subject in CSEC, with a grade three! Trust me, it felt like a grade one to me. On the day when results became available, I thought it best to message her with my grades and share my heartfelt gratitude.

When it came down to her grades, she managed to attain four grade one's, and five grade two's. I got two grade one's, seven grade two's and one grade three. In my opinion, Renicia felt superior to me. I took offense to her arrogance, because in my mind I wrote more subjects which gave me more credit.

To add insult to injury, she then started spewing a narrative that she was more intelligent than me. What made it worse, was that she was saying it to my face around other people. I will pause right here to let you know that I am one of the most competitive persons you will ever meet. Most of my competition is with myself to become a better person every day, as I strive towards living the life of my dreams #LivingMyBestLife.

Renicia and I were a part of the same cohort at CPCE. She was a Math major and English Minor and I was an English Major and Science minor. In her first semester, she got only A's and B's and my girl was on top of the world. In that semester I got B's, C's, one D and a F. My grades only further increased her feeling of superiority towards me. But hear this part now: I finished college when I was scheduled to in 2017, but she never finished until a year after due to her failing two final courses.

Upon realizing that she was not graduating with me, she started boiling down to low gravy. The moral of the story here is that the race is not for the swift, but for those who can endure it to the end. Even the Bible says when you humble yourself you will be exalted. To this day, I continue to excel in the various areas of my life especially academically #SlightShade.

We started worshipping together after all the main worshippers at church got married, one migrated to the United States and the other joined her husband's church in another village. The other elders in the worship team decided to drop out so most times it was only her and I worshipping.

She used to back me up because her confidence was still low in this area but oh, how life has changed. I want to fast forward to a defining moment in our relationship which really showed me how genuine her intentions were for me.

On December 17th 2020, we had the following conversation:

> **R:** Hey, I wanted to ask you something?
>
> **J:** Hey yes go ahead. *(Hearts starts racing)*
>
> **R:** Do you currently struggle with watching pornography (gay porn, masturbation)?
>
> **J:** *(Hearts starts racing, adrenaline rush kicks in, wondering if I should lie to her because how could she know?)* Before I answer your question I want to ask you what led you to ask this question.

R: I had a dream about you... Idk if God is using me to tell you something. This isn't anything for me to go back to tell anyone EVER. Just me, you and God.

J: On that note, yes I have been struggling with it for years and God knows it very hard for me. The shame and guilt is never easy to deal with. Truth is I am struggling with my sexuality and because of that I try to hold onto to God more before I do something I might regret. I felt like God was leading me to talk to someone about this but I have never found the courage to do so. So I know it had to be God who gave you that dream. I was just saying to myself I want to be delivered from this addiction before this year ends. 😭😥😓

R: Okay. I'll tell you the dream.
I was in a room and in the room there were people having sex at different points and I noticed it was gay sex. And right after seeing that I saw you high up and unexpectedly you had a long and hard fall down (falling into sin deeper sin)
I saw you and ran to help u get back up.

This is just a snippet of how the conversation went. We talked a bit more and she shared her own personal struggles with me. From that day, she prayed with me every night and we also studied the word together. She was really my cheerleader and what felt good was that when I was in her presence, I never felt judged nor scorned about my struggles.

To this day we always speak transparently to each other, in hopes of building ourselves up. This is another friendship that I appreciate because she was the first person who I ever shared this side of me with. What this friendship has taught me is that people can change and evolve. When they do, let's give them the permission to, and stop bringing up their past.

Friends are people that you should be able to rely on, trust and honor. I encourage you to define what friendship means to you and when you do find your tribe. Sometimes the people we want for us aren't good for us. Ask God to sift the fakers out like wheat because you DESERVE the BEST on your team #NoSnakeshit!

CHAPTER SIX:

LEW

Takes a deep breath

Have you ever had a friendship that crushed you when it ended? Yea, me too. I dedicate this chapter to a friendship that left me feeling like a shell of a person. So, where do I begin? It was September of 2015 when I met one of the most beautiful women in my life.

Her name was Alissa Shonette Lewis (now Williams, but we will get to all of that). We were students at the Cyril Potter College of Education, pursuing our Associate Degree in Education-English. Our class was called PSS1A because we were in year one of two.

Our class representative, Clarissa, was talking about the way we should conduct ourselves as teachers in training, and the discussion someone lead to the topic of conflict. I vividly recall Alissa standing up to say that conflict it is inevitable, so we just have to find a way to work through it.

I was pleasantly surprised at how poised and well-spoken she was, so immediately I decided to pursue a friendship with her. She and I used to take a drop with Penelope Wintz, commonly known as Penny, our big woman friend at college. She was the experienced one and a road girl, but she's a loving and caring person at her core.

At the time, Penny and I were close. We used to talk and laugh a lot and she knew some people I went to school with. After I realised that Penny used to drive, I would get in on a few drops to the line top, so I only had to walk a short distance home.

Alissa lived in the village of Ann's Grove which is located further up the east coast of Demerara. She too used to take a drop with Penny up to Golden Grove then get a back or taxi to take her home. (Penny lived in Belfield which is before Ann's Grove.)

I remember telling myself when I first laid eyes on her that she was going to be my friend, and to this day I wonder if what we had was real. Only God knows but I will say this: I left this situation will lifelong experiences. The first car ride we took with Penny, we introduced ourselves to each other and exchanged Facebook details.

We engaged in small talk until it was time for me to come off at my spot. I quickly went home and searched for her name on Facebook and when it popped up, I immediately clicked the 'Add Friend' option. She accepted the request on the same day. Guess who was all smiles? This guy, because my plan to befriend her was in motion.

At the time I was sitting next to Penny in teacher's training, at the opposite side of the classroom from Alissa. I wanted to change seats but it wasn't that simple. Over time, tension grew between Penny and I, which resulted in us not speaking to each other. This was my perfect opportunity to change seats in class.

Alissa was seated next to the fun crew of the class which consisted of Sarah, Kishona, Giselle, Yvette and Alissa. I inserted myself into this circle of young women and everyone in this group was kind to me except Yvette who preferred that I sit elsewhere. She would move my chair whenever she got the chance. This made me feel really bad, but Alissa would always stand up for me.

Over time my love and admiration grew for Alissa, as we got to know one another. I gathered that she used to attend the school I was attached to as a teacher (Annandale Secondary). She had taken a gap year after high school and then completed a Bachelor's degree in Sociology. She was biracial and a Christian who worked at the Guyana Revenue Authority for some time. You get the picture.

We began sharing ourselves with each other. Yes, I am aware of how that sounds but you know what I mean. With each new detail, I grew closer to her. I was the guy who finished secondary school and started college right after. Alissa was one of the most intellectual persons who I knew at the time. In my opinion, all the lecturers loved her because she carried herself with grace, and was so eloquent in speech #FULLSCORE.

At this time my mom was still supporting me through college, so most days I would go there with between Guyanese $300-$500. Alissa used to roll with big bucks, I cannot say for sure if her mother used to support her during this time or someone else, but she looked fine and financially stable. Eventually we shared numbers on WhatsApp so we would stay in touch. By this time, Yvette had failed out of college because of her poor performance so I had Alissa all to myself. The others in the group didn't matter to me.

The first breakdown in our friendship happened when I found out she had a boyfriend, I was like WHAT! How was this not communicated to me earlier? His name was Paul. That Bitch. A pastor's son but still too wotless for his own good. I remember seeing a picture she shared on Instagram of her shadow at the seawalls and one of the hashtags was #HeTookIt.

I rubbed my eyes to see if I was reading correctly and upon

further investigation, learned that she was taken. Everyone in the group knew I had a big crush on her because my actions said it all. If anyone ever said anything bad about her, I would defend her honor because I took it as my responsibility. To this day I felt like she tolerated me with my childish behaviors because as soon as we left College shit changed drastically between us.

The second breakdown in our friendship occurred when she lied to me by sending me an ultrasound picture claiming that she was pregnant. I was flabbergasted and very concerned for her. I rattled off a series of questions like *Will you keep it? What will your mom say? What does Paul have to say about this? Will he marry you now?* She had a response to each. I was surprised to learn that she had sent the same message to everyone in our group — I thought I was special.

We were all concerned for her. Honestly, I didn't even sleep properly that night because her friendship meant so much to me. I was already thinking of ways to be a supportive friend to her. The next day persons in our group were laughing at me for being so concerned, and for thinking I was the only one who knew the news.

The woman of the hour finally showed up after being missing for days. Apparently, she had a throat infection so the doctor gave her a medical. I stopped talking to her for a few hours because I felt so stupid. The thing is when Alissa laid eyes on me and gave me her undivided attention, I felt seen in a way that I hadn't experienced before, so I was holding on to that.

I remember for her birthday one year she bought ice cream for me because I had no money to do so. Yes, I felt good about that because for me, those moments meant that she cared. Was it all out of love or duty? I still question that.

Upon finishing college life took a bad turn for us. She hooked up with an old guy friend of hers and started becoming very distant. Our messages became more infrequent, and she ruined our Snapchat streak. I was no longer the friend her mother encouraged her to be around.

The type of connection I craved I was being deprived of and what hurt most was that it was clear that she didn't care anymore. My girl was traveling all around Guyana, buying lovely things and posting all about it on WhatsApp status where I could watch.
Ever since our college days, our fallouts (which would always be her fault for sidelining me), always ended with her coming back to me with a sweet apology that would win me over.

Look at this one:

A: Jaredddddddddd babyyyyyyyyy... I'm sorry... I truly am. I'm such a bitch, I was probably ovulating... but sincerely apologize... Ah miss ma babyyyy. Hope you find it in your heart to forgive me man... (three Kissy face emoji's)

J: I really hope you mean this cause our friendship means a lot to me hope it does to you too.

Now watch this part. After we sent some emoji's back and forth, she said:

A: So now that that's overrr, So I been to the pageant last night

(She then went on to deliver some juicy gossip to me that I indulged in because I was truly a messy person).

What I didn't realise, is that this was a pattern because I always forgave her. People say that distance shows how strong a relationship is and where I erred was that I didn't make my boundaries clear in ours. We were both operating on assumptions and in this pattern of a cause-and-effect relationship. Alissa knew that I liked her more than a friend but she never confronted me about it and I never admitted it either. We friend-zoned each other.

Post CPCE I felt like I was doing all the work in the friendship, while she took a more laid-back approach. Suddenly, I knew nothing new about her. We barely went out together anymore and when we did it was always an issue with her boyfriend (now Husband). Not to be messy, but this is my interpretation of how the events unfolded. Lionel was all she cared about. My girl only moved with cars now — she was on another level and I was beneath her.

I couldn't afford the lifestyle she had and wanted. I was now a thing of her past. She only kept in contact with me out of obligation and now our conversations were no longer deep. She got married in 2019 to this bitch and guess what? I was invited until I wasn't.

Word is she ended up getting married at General Register Office with a small gathering afterward that to this day she claimed never happened. This crushed my soul because I secretly wished it was us getting married. This was the first time murderous thoughts filled my mind for her man. The other thing that hurt me was we could pass for relatives, and we sound very similar so sometimes it feels like she married my doppelganger.

I flew into a rage before she got married and blocked her from all my social media accounts including deleting our WhatsApp conversation. I kept the images of us in my Google photos album. Would you believe that it took her about a month to notice that I had blocked her? She tried calling my phone at one point, and I refused to answer her call. I used to do a toxic thing where I would re-add her number on WhatsApp to see if she could see my status and guess what? She never deleted my number which felt good to me for a while.

Eventually I would realise that she was living her best life without me while I was stuck in the past, so I would block her again. I remember one time I blocked her for months and then unblocked her on her birthday to wish her well. She responded, *"Thanks baby, I love you so much,"* but her actions sure as hell didn't feel like love.

Our months of not talking felt like exile to me. I was depressed but most persons around me didn't even realise. I pretended like I was fine. To most, I am always the happy bubbly guy but deep down I was broken. Yet another failed connection with a female whom I loved and cherished.

Allow me to side bar quickly for a moment. You see, this feeling of betrayal and unrequited love was all too familiar to me. I had a huge crush on a girl from my church. *(She knows herself so if you're reading this big up!)* We used to talk every day on Twitter about everything and when we met up in person it was all smiles and blushes. Now here's another fun fact about me: when I love, I love hard until it hurts to keep it to myself. I decided to share my feelings with her and this is how it went on <u>April 29th 2014:</u>

J: I need to talk to you... Good morning... but waiting on the buildup of courage.

R: Build up on courage for what!!!?!! Is just me, start talk, hear what you send DMs and I will read it when I come home from UG.

J: Hey R, I got the buildup of courage now, this is just between me and you. Well since a while now I really wanted to talk to you don't know how to say this but I will, since a while now I have and still do admire you. I really don't know how it happen but R I find you fun, jolly, and weird in a special kind of way real fan of misfits and living the #116 life. Peculiar in every way and in everything you do and I can go on and on... every night I would dream of you and I would even pray for you and because of the last dream I had and the last prayer I prayed I really feel led and motivated to tell you how I feel about you. I would really like to know R if you feel the same way about me or if you are even ready to be in a relationship.

And I know you are 2 yrs. older than me but please please let this be between us. I don't know if you feel the same way but now my mind is relieved. I'll be here waiting for your response. As much as I want u to say yes 2 me, it is up 2 u. U have the winning cards in your hand here!!

R: lol hahahaha :D this made me laugh :D and ok this will be between me and you :D only, wouldn't even tell Nets (her other sister). And I don't like younger guys than me sorry lol and relationship? No I can't handle that at all now too busy with UG. Plus I don't have the time to like anyone lol :D don't let this make you feel bad or anything alright and don't let dis make us stop talk either. Lol hahahahaha you really made me laugh dis afternoon though Jared :D

Now let the record show that we did stop talking after a while. We both made it weird to the point where she would lash out at me for simple things. The thing that hurt me most was that within months she was in a relationship with a guy who she is now married to. The gag is both her and Alissa got married in the same year. People, you can imagine what this did to my mental health. #Drained #Exhausted #FedupofLoveandLife

I think the many rejections that I received from females led to my attraction to guys thinking that maybe they wouldn't reject me but the gag is I have just never been in a relationship to anything to a day like this! Yes, you read that right. Even if I like someone I would never tell them because my past traumas of pouring out my heart and getting rejected come up.

Now back to Lew. I remember someone came up to me and said, "what's up with you and Alissa I don't see any post or anything," I related to them what happened and how she has changed and the person began relating their friend's experience of her and how she became distant with them too and this was confirmation to me that all of this wasn't just in my head.

Months after I built up the courage to send her a voice note on WhatsApp about how her actions affected me and she agreed and said she doesn't have time to fix any relationship not in those exact words but those were her sentiments. After then I made up my mind that that was the last straw, I remember seeing her a day while I was going to UG.

We ran and hugged each other but this time it was different. We had both changed and we knew it. We were no longer those kids from college but adults figuring out our place in the world. We reconnected for a bit but it felt forced so I just stopped texting back. Up until this day, we haven't spoken. I once read a post that she made which I assumed was aimed at former friends like me. It said:

> *Would you take the garbage out of the can after you have dumped it? Then why would you add back that number?*

That stung but I had to accept the past for what it was. I was intent on finding my learning moments and using them to thrust me farther into my destiny. I took two main things away from this toxic friendship. The first being the importance of establishing boundaries from the onset. The second is that I should always express how I truly feel. Blurred lines cause confusion and heartache in the end.

I have nothing but all love for LEW. Yes, I am still working through some trauma because my girl appears to be living her best life. To this day she is CLOSE friends with someone we used to gossip about. Sometimes I wonder if those two people obeah her because neither of them wanted me in her life. They succeeded. They can keep her all to themselves. I will have my moment. This book is just the beginning.

It's like I mentioned before: I am always dramatic first and logical second, I remember listening to the Chole x Halle songs, "Thinkin' About Me" and "Who Knew." These songs had an impact on my emotions and I placed Lew on blast where I uploaded pictures of Us and one of our mutual friends where I blocked out her face with emoji's and I went in.

The same friend that she is now besties with, screenshot those posts and sent them to her. Lew's response to my statuses was very disrespectful. She even attacked my sexuality but I guess it was all fair game. Subsequently, I blocked the Judas that sent her the screen shots. To this day,

Lew feels like the one that got away.

Today I acknowledge my toxicity during that time. I didn't know I was me. I was depressed and suffering from very low self-esteem. I put too much on Lew without trying to fix myself. Today I am way better off. Hell, I got a BOOK!

As this chapter closes I want you to write down a list of qualities you want in your friends, and what you will do if they don't meet them. I have come to learn that some people are just in our lives for a short period of time to teach us something and that's what Lew was to me. I am grateful for the lessons learnt.

CHAPTER SEVEN:
Be Thou Forgiven

Matthew 18:21-22 KJV says,

"Then came Peter to him, and said, Lord, how oft shall my brother sin against me, and I forgive him? Till seven times? Jesus saith unto him, I say not unto thee, until seven times: but, until seventy times seven."

This portion of scripture gets me every time because I don't think that Jesus meant for us to count the times we have forgiven others until it amounts to four hundred and ninety. I believe it was an expression for us to understand that forgiveness is a lifestyle — we should constantly choose to forgive others who have wronged us. This analogy doesn't hurt me because when I think of the number of times I have sinned against God's word and done my own thing, yet His grace and love for me knows no bound.

Romans 8:38-39 says:

"For I am persuaded, that neither death, nor life, nor angels, nor principalities, nor powers, nor things present, nor things to come, nor height, nor depth, nor any other

creature, shall be able to separate us from the love of God, which is in Christ Jesus our Lord."

These two verses are evidence that nothing or no one can separate us from the deep love that God has for us. I want you to think about the person in your life that Loves you the most, now think about that person you love the most in life, well God's love for you is greater, his Love is genuine and pure that's why it's called *agape* love.

Many Christians with flawed theology will try to make you feel like your past is beyond forgiveness, or make you feel like your lifestyle exempts you from it. That is all a lie. You are God's most prized possession. The Bible says we are the head and not the tail, called out, peculiar and — my favorite — a royal priesthood.

Knowing this, why are you allowing people to treat you poorly? When we experience God's deep love, we begin to understand who we are in Him because outside of God we are totally different. God's love lifts a standard in our life. It transforms and renews our spirit, which results in higher our self-esteem.

Oh, they said you changed since you came to know God. Let them know this is just a side effect of believing the word of God, and self-realization. Before even writing this book I had to experience it for myself. What I have come to learn in my twenty-three years of living is that my identity is found in God's grace. In Him I am known. So, to anyone looking for a partner I encourage you to stay in God, and you will find your Godly match.

DAD

My father, Kenneth Miller has hurt me the most in my life. His absence alone felt like gross rejection. I didn't and still don't feel like the son he wanted. As I mentioned in Chapter 1, my mother usually says that she was happiest while having me. She lacked nothing and my father treated her like a queen.

I often wonder what his thoughts were after seeing me for the first time, and his thoughts about me now. Am I the first-born son he envisioned? I sometimes wonder if because I don't carry his last name he feels I am not a true embodiment of his seed. I know for sure that I am his because we love curried chicken and have ugly toe nails (lol).

My father never laid hands on me or talked to me harshly but his actions cut deeper than any physically wound could. He said yes to every request made, but never came through with any. He is surely not a man of his word. On Father's Day I am most insecure because while many people are posting about their dad, I have a deadbeat one that I have hidden from the world. Every time someone asked me about him, I would cut the conversation short by being direct and my body language would change to indicate my contempt and insecurity.

I remember my father didn't contribute in paying my CSEC fees. I asked him for Guyanese $5000 when I was finishing college and to this day, I haven't received this money. He is also a man of few words so he doesn't know how to carry a conversation or maybe that is just with me.

Still, what hurt me the most is that Mom had to take him to court to pay child support for my sister, brother and I. That felt like a low blow to me that we had to go to that extent, because if you made kids, it is your responsibility and yours only to take care of them! I remember my mom sharing a comment that he made to her that because they ended their relationship the children will suffer as a result.

My father was always a married man. I remember his wife saying once that her kids never drank black tea in their life. Well, let me tell you I have drank black tea more times that I can count and it is one of the best teas out there. (By "black tea" I mean tea bag in case you were wondering.) His wife was very sometimes -ish. One time she would treat you the best, and another it was like a demon had possessed her and she was filled with contempt and resentment.

Sometimes I feel like she had insecurities because my siblings and I are smarter than her kids and look better too.

How could these kids who are not even being taken care of by their father still manage to be well-fed, look great and educated?

My dear father I FORGIVE YOU. I no longer hold you accountable for the wrongs you have committed against me.

Sometimes I think that my attraction to men stems from this fragmented relationship with my dad. I feel I was seeking out in guys what my father should have been for me, such as a provider, protector and friend. I choose to forgive you for my own peace of mind. Lastly, I remember one thing as a way to get back at him I planned to pass him straight on the road.

It was the funeral of a close family friend. My father was standing outside of the church and I knew his usual behavior was to boast about our success, so I took the opportunity to hurt him. I planned my attack and when the service was over, I walked confidently out of the church side-eyeing him. The moment came when he was expecting me to acknowledge him. I struck then and passed him not only like a stranger but like an English Literature exam — quick and easy.

Did I achieve my expected results? HELL YES, because my mom called me later that afternoon to say my father told her that I passed him straight on the road, "not a hello." I of course denied it and swore on everything that I didn't but I had to hold out because I needed him to feel the hurt I carried due to his absence from my life.

It's like Michael Todd says, he is a "Father Unaware." I forgive him because he just didn't know any better. Sometimes I wonder if my father still holds this incident against me. If he doesn't, daddy I am sorry.

MOM

I feel like because my mother was very stressed and depressed during my siblings and I's childhood, she used to take out that anger, fatigue and frustration on us. I remember my small sister, Brianna and I getting licks with an electrical cord because the room was not cleaned. Mom locked the door to trap us in the room and the thrashing was sound.

I remember a phase when she had a conveyer belt that she used to beat us whenever we fell out of line. What this did to me was mess with my mind. I started living in fear of my mother because at any moment I could have inadvertently done something to set her off. I was walking on egg shells.

One of my most notable thrashings happened when I was in fourth form. It was a Saturday and I was preparing to go to math's lessons. My mother asked me a question but my response was deemed disrespectful. She beat me so badly that I remember lying on the floor hollering for mercy and her response was, *"If yuh get blackout I will throw water on you."*

Even as I write this my heart feels heavy and the tears are flowing because I interpreted those words and actions as hatred towards me. Over time the fear I had for her metamorphosed into full blown hatred which was evident in my subtle rebellion and the tone in which I spoke to her. There was also a time when my response to my mom caused her to bore me with an eating fork.

The hardest part about all of this is that to this day my mom has not apologized to me for the pain she inflicted upon me physically and emotionally. She holds out that she did the best she could. I think pride is what is holding her back from saying those simple and meaningful words to me, because she knows I deserve them. I would often tell her that I need therapy for the trauma she has inflicted upon me and she laughs at this.

I remember while we were preparing our house for Christmas 2020, we ended up in a heated argument over how she treated me and this triggered a rage in me. Truth is, my mom, like most Guyanese moms, are over protective of their kids. They are unlikely to allow us to individuate and express ourselves the best way we can. Many times I did not feel like a reflection or expression of either of my parents.

To my dear mother: I know you did the best you could have with my siblings and I. I know my actions did not always reflect my appreciation because I do think that you could have done better. You are such a strong woman and I feel like sometimes you allowed life to happen to you. I guess you got tired of fighting every opposition.

You and I are both alphas — we lead and command. We are so much alike and I feel that's why we clash ever so often. I LOVE YOU with my entire heart and I cannot imagine my life without you.

I am a reflection of ME. I have a voice and my voice deserves to be heard. I feel like for most of my life I was silenced and smothered, but now I'm learning how to breathe and speak at my own will. I truly look forward to moving out of my mom's house because I feel this will make her see me as an adult. I know that I couldn't choose the mother God gave to me so I have to love her for what she did — right and wrong.

Mother, I FORGIVE YOU.

To the following persons who so deeply hurt me:

LEW, I FORGIVE YOU for hurting me so deeply that I don't know if I will ever love a woman again.

Izzy, I FORGIVE YOU for not wishing me a happy twenty second birthday and for not congratulating me on finishing or graduating from UG. I don't know if it is because I am younger than you and my life has accelerated faster than yours, but I want you to know I still do cherish our moments of shared music and gossiping.

Jude, I FORGIVE YOU for not congratulating me on graduating from UG. The thing is, I congratulated you when it was your turn. I wrote an entire post for you on WhatsApp, and I meant it. I know you have always looked at me as your competition, or as a standard for how high you could soar, but I will not apologize for the grace of God on my life.

My step-sister Shenika, I FORGIVE YOU for calling me an "Aunty Man," because you didn't like my rude comments on the photo you posted on Facebook. I should not have commented it there.

I forgive all of the church folks that hurt me, every bully from school, and my village. I FORGIVE YOU ALL.

Most of all, I FORGIVE ME for both the things I could have controlled, and the ones I could not have controlled. I FORGIVE ME for my part in every pain and trauma that I suffered. I FORGIVE ME for it all!

I FORGIVE ME.

The thing with forgiveness, is that it's for you and no one else. I have learnt that some people will never apologize for the hurt and pain they caused you. So, why wait for them, when you can forgive you, and move on? Forgiveness is a gift many seek but only a few can receive. Give yourself the permission to forgive and set your soul free. You got purpose, baby!

INTERLUDE

I have always been told that I make people feel good. I remember a classmate commenting that most fat people that she had met were very funny. I rejected that image of being the fat, black, funny guy. I mistook my ability to make people laugh for a flaw. Over time, I came to realise that my joy is a weapon.

I read somewhere that Black Joy is activism and I agree. Sometimes there are so many things pressed against us, that our joy is the one thing that we can use as active resistance.

Stop walking around wearing your problems on your face. You don't have to look like what you have been through. Joy is internal. The Joy I have, the world didn't give it to me so they can't take it. I believe this with every fiber of my being.

The next five chapters of my book are dedicated to encourage you to live the life of your dreams from the best book I have ever read — the BIBLE. NO, you do not have to close this book. Trust me, you will be inspired and impacted because I will make real life application with each topic. I know I have been blessed with the spirit of encouragement, so I pray that these words flow right into your spirit as you read. May your passion and purpose be ignited and may your appetite for more become opened.

You may be asking yourself why I named this book *"By Grace through Faith."* I did so because I am where I am today because of God's grace — I could not have done it without Him. He is my source. God has lifted my family and I out of the rut and it only gets better from here.

At twenty-three I already have a Bachelor's degree and five years of teaching experience. I have coached teachers (all of whom were older than me), and I lecture part-time at the Cyril Potter College of Education. I gained prominence from my exposure as a presenter at the Guyana Learning Channel Trust. Finally, I am considered an elder in my church community because of my contributions to several departments such as Children Ministry, Sunday School, Youth Ministry, Pastoral Team and Worship Ministry.

It is safe to say that I am favored greatly by God and I do not take this for granted. Uncommon favor follows me. I am a shining star whose light will never burn out because I am powered by an eternal source.

I was the first in my house to leave the country when I went to Jamaica for a conference and did a one-week missionary trip. I was the first sibling to get a visitor's visa to go to the United States of America. I was the first to complete a tertiary degree (CPCE) and of course, the first to write a book.

Many people say to me that I have done a lot for my age. They then go on to share that when they were my age they were still trying to figure their life out. As for me, I have always known what I wanted for my life. My goals have given me stability during the very rough chapters of my life.

From very early on in my life, I knew I wanted to become an Educator because I admired my teachers greatly and the work they did. Teaching has always come naturally to me. I am a gifted public speaker because of my engaging personality. People always want to hear me speak or whenever they see me on a platform they are intrigued to know what I will say.

I stand boldly in this moment — flaws and all — bearing my soul raw in this book because I believe that my story and encouragement will lift you out of that place you are in and get you back into the game. So, hear me out and let me know what you think because like Michaela Jae I got *Something to Say*.

CHAPTER 8:
Are you Fighting For your Dreams?

I once came across a definition of the word Dream from the Emily Dickinson Lexicon which says; *"The thought or series of thoughts of a person in sleep. We apply dream, in the singular, to a series of thoughts, which occupy the mind of a sleeping person, in which he imagines he has a view of real things or transactions."*

Another definition of Dream from Study Light says, *"A dream is a series of thoughts not under the command of reason, and hence wild and irregular."*

In scripture, dreams were sometimes impressions on the minds of sleeping persons, made by divine agency. God came to Abimelech in a dream. Joseph was warned by God in a dream.

In Proverbs 29:18 KJV the Bible says, *"Where there is no vision, the people perish: but he that keepeth the law, happy is he."*

Do you know what God's vision for your life is? If not, it's time to do some introspection. The Bible tells us that without vision we cannot survive nor thrive. Therefore, having vision is necessary for us to exist and prosper. When we hold fast to the vision that God has given us for our life, the joy and happiness that comes with it is irreplaceable.

Vision gives us a reason to live. The devil will try to use different life situations as distractions from you focusing on your vision but keep on keeping on. The visions and dreams that God gave to you are yours but you have a responsibility to fight for them.

I want you to take a moment and write down the things you want to see happen in your life. You could use a piece of paper or grab your journal to make these notes. What are the instructions and goals that God gave you for your life?

You may be wondering how do I know when it's God? Well, let me use myself as an example. I never in all my life thought I would be a published author. One day I was sitting around in the early pandemic days, and suddenly this idea dropped in my spirit that I should write a book. I laughed to myself because in my mind I thought how can I?

The more I resisted this idea, the more God begin to impress it upon my heart so I had to sit and think about it. If God is showing it to me, if He says I can and must do it, who am I to question His authority? The Bible did say that His thoughts and ways are higher than mine.

He is surely a man to his word he can and never will lie to us. God sees us as our highest selves, even when we feel broken and distant from him. That's where His Grace comes in. Trust God's knowledge about you even when you don't trust you.

I want to expand on a few points the extraordinary Michael Todd made in his message *"Mark My Words"* he said:

1. Vision is most valuable

I want you to think of vision as a golden nugget locked within your spirit. It is your task to unleash your vision into the world, so that it can manifest and bear fruit for you and the other people attached to it. Beware of foul people and spirits that may try to steal this nugget from you. Remember that your vision is unique to you.

2. Vision must be a value

Do you value the vision that God has given to you? If you do you will work harder to achieve it regardless of any turmoil that may follow. I find it weird that when one is in alignment with God's vision for their life, that is when they begin to face the most adversity. There is a scripture in the Bible that helped me to understand why,

1 Corinthians 16:9 KJV *"For a great door and effectual is opened unto me, and there are many adversaries."* So, the next time you face great adversities just take a look and see

how close you are to your goal. It will make you want to push back against those adversities.

3. Vision is always vertical

Vision comes from God. In my quiet moments, I sit and ask God for ideas for what I'm working on and better believe He gives me one. It makes sense because God is the author of creativity. Look at the World He made in seven days! Look at you reading my words! You are one of His greatest masterpieces, so don't settle for less or take any BS from anyone.

4. Vision is God's Investment

The thing about this investment is that God gets something great out of your obedience to honor the vision He gave to you. In turn, you get the life of your dreams — living in purpose as your highest self. Many don't reach to this level of success because they are too comfortable where they are at.

They are afraid to step into the unknown. The unknown isn't such a bad place after all, because it's the unknown that unleashes greater potential you never knew existed within yourself. You can bet on God but the greater question is, can God bet on you?

5. Vision needs a vehicle

You are the vehicle God is using to carry His visions out in the earth. As such, we are only stewards of God's vision, so stop taking full credit for it. I truly believe that when we understand that we have a mandate to leave the world in a better state than we encountered it, we will have accomplished our goal in life. Even if it means impacting ten or two people. You have a duty and you are replaceable. I did not stutter — you are replaceable.

What isn't replaceable, is your potential to make an impact. That can never be removed or taken away from you. If I resign from my current teaching position, another teacher will soon fill that vacancy BUT the impact that I would have made on my colleagues, parents and students could not be replicated.

I want you to carry this with you in everything you do. Ask yourself: am I being purposeful? Am I taking up space in the roles I occupy?

6. God gives vision in Valleys

I remember reading Yvonne Orji's book where she testified about the Holy Spirit showing up in one of her low moments, and sharing His plans for her life. Look at God! She is living in that now. I believe God gives us vision in the low moments because we are very vulnerable then and looking for hope a reason to keep on going and growing. I can attest to the fact that everything God has promised me, has started to become a reality...simply by His grace.

7. Vision must be visible and vocal

When you have a vision that you are working towards, you need to be practical. One question I have learnt to constantly ask myself as I pursue my dreams is: what are the practical steps I need to take to make this dream a reality? We need to come to the point where we document every step and track our progress as we work to achieve our goals.

Another important point to consider is this: what are the potential barriers that can deter or delay your progress? In terms of being vocal, we need to begin speaking our vision and dreams to life. I call this *manifesting*. One thing I do is attach a Bible verse to my dreams and vision for my life. This serves as a reminder to God of His promises to me, and as I have said before God is a man of His word.

8. Vision is God's view

The thing is your view is limited to what you can see. Meanwhile, God has an aerial and multidimensional view of your life. He is the author of time, so His vision spans beyond our earthly dimension. All God needs from you now is active faith through obedience, like Abraham. That man truly trusted God with all of his heart.

We can still see his boundless blessings that still exist today. It's like my associate pastor always says, *"Trust God where you can't trace Him."* One of my favorite worship songs, "Way Maker" by Michael W. Smith says, *"even when we can't see God He's working / Even when we can't feel it, He's working / He NEVER stops working.*

9. Vision has versions

At first I did not fully understand what this meant but as I studied it more it began to make sense. The version of the vision we ultimately receive speaks to how hard we work for it. Some people go ahead with God's vision partly and expect to reap the full benefits. You can only receive the full benefits when you go all the way. So, push past insecurities, fears, doubts and launch out greater into your destiny, because it is waiting on your YES. Your best self is waiting on you to reach the cusp of self-actualization.

10. Vision is for victory

I don't know about you but something about this word just sets my soul on fire. I love victory and as a believer, I need you to claim that victory is your portion. Like the song says, you wear the victor's crown. When God gives you a vision, it is ultimately for your success. As Christians, we are supposed to be leading industries with innovation and integrity.

Finally, let's examine a familiar portion of scripture with the disciple Peter and Jesus in Matthew 14: 22-33. Here we see that Jesus instructs his disciples to go onto a ship and wait for Him while He goes to pray in the mountains. Verse 24 tells us that the ship was caught in some terrible wind, and Jesus walked on the water. As He was approaching the boat, the disciples saw Him and cried out of fear thinking that it was a spirit.

Let's pause right here for a minute because these disciples were with Jesus for a while now and yet they were afraid and blinded by fear. Fear is a destiny stealer so bind that spirit up in the name of Jesus. Many times we allow fear to prevent us from seeing God's vision for our life the way He showed it to us. Jesus encouraged His disciples. I believe God is using me to encourage you as well. Do not fear. It is your God who gave you those wild and huge dreams and visions in the first place, so your God will guide you through the process of making them a reality.

Peter playing a bravado asked Jesus to bid him to come out on the water and Jesus told him to come. Peter stepped out in faith and began doing what was unnatural. God will do the unnatural in your life if you only step out in faith upon his instructions. God is a protocol-breaker. The laws of our realm do not define nor confine him.

Trust God to do a new thing in your life. Tasha Cobbs said in her song "I'm Getting Ready": *Eyes haven't seen / And ears haven't heard / The kind of blessings / That's about to fall on me.*

As soon as the wind became boisterous, Peter lost faith and as a result of his unbelief, he began to sink. You need to keep your eyes on Jesus. He is your present help. When you are greeted with adversity, keep your eyes on the One who said He will be an adversary to your adversity.

FIGHT FOR YOUR DREAMS! Jesus saved Peter and took him back safely to the ship. I encourage you to be of great courage and faith. This new version of you requires unorthodox faith. It requires the kind of faith that shakes mountains and upsets systems. All barriers must bow to your faith in God.

CHAPTER 9:
Being Distinguished by Distinction

Dreams

Hold fast to dreams
For if dreams die
Life is a broken-winged bird
That cannot fly.

Hold fast to dreams
For when dreams go
Life is a barren field
Frozen with snow.

BY: LANGSTON HUGHES

This is one of my favorite poems because it speaks volumes, Life is so unpredictable hence you should not waste another minute living below your highest potential. It's time to make an action plan to turn your life around, the life of your dreams awaits.

We commit creative suicide when we do not step into who we are fully, imagine killing your potentials before you even gave them a chance. Many people lead boring lives not because they are boring people but because they are not doing the things that light their soul on fire. They are not doing the thing that makes them eager to rise from their bed each day.

Your dreams will begin to make sense when you know God through his word. The Bible says in Habakkuk 22:2 KJV: *"And the LORD answered me, and said, Write the vision, and make it plain upon tables, that he may run that readeth it."*

It's time to grab a piece of paper or your journal and write down every vision and dream for your life. Ensure that they are as clear as day. When they are clear, you will understand the mandate in your life to do better. Think of your vision as your baby — you must nurture it for a time and then comes the birthing process. The birthing can be difficult but when you finish you will find that all the pain you endured was worth it. God will give you double for your trouble — you better believe that.

Let's examine the story of Joseph, the bonafide dreamer. His story highlights some points that we can learn from. We were all born with dreams it just takes us time to understand and articulate them. What do you do when the dream is bigger than you, your family, your community and your country?

I repeat: what God is about to do in your life through your

obedience to him is unheard of. It will blow the mind of every witness.

Genesis chapter 37: 3 says: *"Now Israel loved Joseph more than all his children, because he was the son of his old age: and he made him a coat of many colours."*

Israel's (Jacob's) love for Joseph is representative of God's favor upon your life. Remember He leaves the ninety-nine for the one. I want you to know that you are that one. He is calling you out so don't be afraid. People will judge you but when God begins to prosper you, they will want a piece.

Verses 3 and 4 go on to describe Joseph's dreams but notice what is said at the end of verse 8: *"And they hated him yet the more for his dreams, and for his words."* This shows us that we need to be very careful about who we share our dreams with because many people only pretend to be happy for us. As I often say, jealousy and envy are feelings felt by all. I have experienced them quite a few times but I combat them by choosing to reminisce on what God has done for me.

My brothers and sisters, I encourage you to stay in your lane and focus on the course set before you, as you press towards the mark of the higher calling in Christ (Philippians 3:14 KJV).

In verse 18 Joseph's brothers plotted against him. This shows us that people will hate and despise you for daring to dream but keep on dreaming!

Dear parents, encourage your children to dream and dream big. Do not project your frustrations or fears onto them, by assuming what they can and cannot do. I am always amazed that young children dream audaciously, but the older they get their ability to dream decreases.

This shouldn't be. The more we grow, the more our appetite should increase. Every time I travel to another country, I become hungry for betterment in my life, because I become aware that there are more options available to me beyond the borders of Guyana.

When I realized that I wanted to become an artist I said excitedly at the dinner table, *"I'm going to be a Broadway star."* My mom responded, *"because your cousin John went on Broadway you want to do the same."* I felt so dismissed that I immediately regretted sharing my dream with her. I did not confide in her or anybody else for years. I began to perceive limits and have self-doubt.

Now, I dare to trust what God sees in me. Do you trust what God sees in you?

In Verse 19 Joseph's brother's mocked him by saying, *"Behold, this dreamer cometh."* People will try to mock you but do not stop dreaming! I have always heard the saying, "he who laughs last does laugh the best." I decree and declare that your enemies will not be able to laugh at your demise instead they will be dumbfounded by your success, in Jesus' mighty name.

In Verses 23 and 24 his brothers deceived him and took his coat from him, and I say to you now watch out for the people you have CLOSEST to you. There may very well be a deceiver in the midst. His brothers sold him for twenty pieces of silver. Who is willing to sell you for their success or gain?

As we jump across to verse 36 we see 'purpose in motion.' Just when his brothers thought they were doing Joseph a bad deed that would end him, God turned up the volume and use this very dark situation to catapult Joseph into his ministry and destiny.

In Chapter 39 and verse 2 we see that Joseph's circumstances did not hinder the plans of God for his life: *"And the LORD was with Joseph, and he was a prosperous man; and he was in the house of his master the Egyptian."* In the name of Jesus, it does not matter what wicked plans your enemies have for you. They will not stop you from prospering, in Jesus' mighty name! Somebody shout AMEN and receive it!

In verse 3 Joseph starts being noticed for being prosperous, *"And his master saw that the LORD was with him, and that the LORD made all that he did to prosper in his hand."* I wonder how his brothers felt about this?

It continues in verses 5, *"And it came to pass from the time that he had made him overseer in his house, and over all that he had, that the LORD blessed the Egyptian's house for Joseph's sake; and the blessing of the LORD was upon all that he had in the house, and in the field."*

On that note, I will encourage you to protect your anointing because some people are just there to drain you. Before our breakthrough, the enemy fights us from attaining it. When we are walking in our breakthrough, he comes again to try and remove us from our place. This is why our integrity needs to ALWAYS be on one hundred!

It's like Yvonne Orji said in her book, *"Don't let your talent write a check your character can't cash."* Can your character stand the test of fire? Can it endure the fire? Because the more you are elevated in life you will face different devils with different faces.

In verse 8 Joseph was tested. What is admirable is how he refused to give into sin, even when no one else was looking. It's not about doing the right thing when others are looking. Can you do the right thing when no one is checking on you?

*"And she caught him by his garment, saying, 'Lie with me':
and he left his garment in her hand, and fled, and got him
out."* This was an obstacle in Joseph's path but he kept his
integrity, and he was duly rewarded. In verse twenty he was
placed in prison. This happened to be one of his lowest
moments. He experienced the pit and was exalted but then
ended up in prison for honoring God. MAKE IT MAKE
SENSE!

Have you ever done right in God's eyes but the consequence
didn't feel good? Yup, I have been there too, but honey, trust
me when I say God will repay you DOUBLE FOR YOUR
TROUBLE.

In verse 21, God shows up for him: *"But the LORD was with
Joseph, and shewed him mercy, and gave him favour in the
sight of the keeper of the prison."* The thing is when you are
blessed, you're blessed.

Now watch our God in action in verse 23, *"The keeper of the
prison looked not to anything that was under his hand;
because the LORD was with him, and that which he did,
the LORD made it to prosper."* Joseph. Still. Prospered. At his
lowest, God was still with him. If you are going through a
rough patch now God is there with you. Call upon Him and
watch His power and love reach you there and lift you out of
the rut.

In Chapter 40, verse 5, an opportunity for Joseph gifts to be at work is created: *"And they dreamed a dream both of them, each man his dream in one night, each man according to the interpretation of his dream, the butler and the baker of the king of Egypt, which were bound in the prison."*

In verse 23 another disappointment hit Joseph. By this time, this feeling of being wronged and forgotten must have been very familiar to him. The chief butler who was supposed to remember him forgot him after he got his breakthrough.

You may feel forgotten by God but I want you to know that God knows the number of hairs you have on your head and he only made one you. This feeling in itself is a distraction to what God wants to do in your life. He knows your name my brother and sister so don't lose hope.

Chapter 41 *(wow, look how far we have come and Joseph still hasn't received his breakthrough)* verse 1 shows us that two years went by and he was still in prison. Yet, he never let go of his faith in God. In verse 8 they brought all of the magicians of Egypt to interpret the king's dream because it was NOT their assignment, it was Joseph's.

Declare with me: I will not miss my assignment in this season of my life in Jesus' mighty name.

In verse 9 Joseph's time came to be revealed. Look at how his name is being called in the presence of a powerful man. Right now, your name is being called in front of powerful people who have the power to change your life according to God's will! It is not them but the power of God in you working through them for your good.

In verse 14 Joseph had to change his garment and make himself presentable in order to fully show up for his assignment: *"Then Pharaoh sent and called Joseph, and they brought him hastily out of the dungeon: and he shaved himself, and changed his raiment, and came in unto Pharaoh."*

The place where God is taking you, requires some change in behavior. The breakthrough is at a higher level which requires a higher YOU. Don't despise the meaningful shedding that is happening in your life, whether it be with friends, family members, classmates, coworkers or even with yourself. Don't fight the change — embrace it. Some parts of who you are must change to match where God is taking you.

Now, I want us to observe Joseph's response in verse 16, *"And Joseph answered Pharaoh, saying, It is not in me: God shall give Pharaoh an answer of peace."* Notice how it is not pompous nor filled with pride. Instead, he acknowledged the God that is about to do a great work in his life. Many times I marvel at Christians who call upon God for everything and roll tight with Jesus until He elevates them.

Suddenly they are afraid to acknowledge Him and give Him His due credit. They are hoarders of God's glory. If you fall into this category, I say to you be careful because the same God that exalts, humbles. God needs to know that when our moment to shine and have a platform presents itself, we will openly share this moment with Him, even if it makes us look crazy in the eyes of man. The tide will always turn in your favor because our times are in God's hands period!

In verse 33 *(I call it Promotion Time)*, Joseph is being distinguished, set apart and honoured: *"Now therefore let Pharaoh look out a man discreet and wise, and set him over the land of Egypt."* In verses 39 to 42 Joseph is being clothed in excellence, he is being distinguished by distinction:

39 And Pharaoh said unto Joseph, Forasmuch as God hath shewed thee all this, there is none so discreet and wise as thou art:

40 Thou shalt be over my house, and according unto thy word shall all my people be ruled: only in the throne will I be greater than thou.

41 And Pharaoh said unto Joseph, See, I have set thee over all the land of Egypt.

⁴² And Pharaoh took off his ring from his hand, and put it upon Joseph's hand, and arrayed him in vestures of fine linen, and put a gold chain about his neck;

Distinction can be simply defined as excellence that sets someone or something apart from others and that is just what God did to Joseph. God did not use his past against him and will not use your past against you it's already thrown in the sea of forgetfulness it's time to MOVE ON. Your moment of distinction awaits!

Verse 46 says that Joseph was thirty years old when he stood before the king. Look how many years had to pass before Joseph got to this point in his life. Be patient, my brothers and sisters. God's words concerning your life will not fall on dry ground and if it does, know that that dryness will respond to the fruitfulness of God.

BET on God, he da one to come through! If you are like me, patience is scarce but over time God has been working on me. Every time I want to get out of hand with Him, he reminds me of Psalm 27:14: *"Wait on the LORD: be of good courage, and he shall strengthen thine heart: wait, I say, on the LORD."*

Every time I read this verse I always ask God why you got to be so LOUD? But it's true. Waiting is the best because when God delivers, you get to partake in His goodness. If you rush it, you will ruin it.

Verse 52 says, *"And the name of the second called he Ephraim: For God hath caused me to be fruitful in the land*

of my affliction." I want you to know right where you suffered or are suffering right now, you will experience God's superimposed blessings for your life.

Finally, in chapter 42 verse 6 Joseph's moment came and he was fully present in it. This is the time when the dream that God had given him came to pass — the same dream the brothers hated. When the time comes even your enemies will play their role in acknowledging your blessings:

"And Joseph was the governor over the land, and he it was that sold to all the people of the land: and Joseph's brethren came, and bowed down themselves before him with their faces to the earth."

Many times when God gives us a dream we think it's all about the NOW but sometimes when God gives vision it's to motivate you to where he is taking you. To get there, they are some hurdles you need to cross. Don't faint nor lose hope. God is there to faithfully carry you through. It's your time TO BE DISTINGUISHED BY DISTINCTION!

CHAPTER 10:
What that Mouth Do?

What are you speaking over the dreams and visions that God gave to you for your life? Let's examine what Jesus said about words in John 6:63 KJV: *It is the spirit that quickeneth; the flesh profiteth nothing: the words that I speak unto you, they are spirit, and they are life."*

Jesus said that his words are life which informs us that words have the ability to cause a change and shift. In Dr. Cindy Trimm's book *Commanding your Morning* she describes words in the following way:

> *"Words released into the atmosphere do not disappear and dissipate. They have no geographical limitations. Words have power, presence and prophetic implications. They create a magnetic force that pulls the manifestation of what speak-good or bad, blessing or cursing-from other realms, regions and dimensions. They are suspended and incubated in the realm of the spirit awaiting the correct time and optimum condition for manifestation."*

If we are not aligning ourselves with Jesus' words, we are not aligning ourselves with Life. Your words are spirit waiting to be manifested in the earth. The Devil cannot do anything with your words unless you allow him to. I always say where you are currently in life is as a result of the words you or other persons spoke over your life years ago.

Stop and I mean *stop* making jokes with your words. For example, *"I bruck." "We are poor people." "Nothing good will come from me."* I remember being in a taxi one time and the driver said to me as we passed a beautiful house made with expensive materials, *"people like me and you could never afford a house like that."* Under my breath I rebuked him in the mighty name of Jesus and said that is not my portion. The problem is many people cannot see further than their problems.

Once we put out words into the atmosphere, the enemy has something to work with because through our speech he hears what is in our hearts and then he plots and plans to bring attacks. The enemy pays close attention to what is coming out of your mouth because he is always looking for ammunition to use against you.

Death Words = Empower the enemy to work against you with your permission.

Words of Life = Empower the ministering angels of God to go to work on your behalf.

I pray that the life Jesus talks about and the life he came to give you would fully manifest itself right now in your life as you read this just say AMEN! In Matthew 12: 34-37 (MSG) says,

""You have minds like a snake pit! How do you suppose what you say is worth anything when you are so foul-minded? It's your heart, not the dictionary, that gives meaning to your words. A good person produces good deeds and words season after season. An evil person is a blight on the orchard. Let me tell you something: Every one of these careless words is going to come back to haunt you. There will be a time of Reckoning. Words are powerful; take them seriously. Words can be your salvation. Words can also be your damnation."

It is clear to us here that there is a connection between our heart and our words, your words reveal your belief system. I will repeat your life is a reflection of the words you have spoken maybe that's why you are suffering the way you are because you claimed that as your narrative.

We have a responsibility to rebuke every narrative that is not in line with God's will for our life. It's time to claim and reclaim the narrative that is in line with your purpose. You are above and never beneath. You are the head and never the tail. You are peculiar. You are a royal priesthood. Everything you touch prospers by the will of God.

If you want to know what someone thinks just listen long enough and you will be able to identify their thoughts and intents, Matthew 12:37 (KJV) says, *"For by thy words thou shalt be justified, and by thy words thou shalt be condemned."* Once we voice our thoughts, we give them permission to manifest and in due time we will be judged by those very words.

I also want to take this time to caution you to be very careful about the words you speak over other people, their children and even your enemies. When I was in secondary school we used to say, "words you speak refer to yourself." This is absolutely true because your words reveal the content of your character and this is what I assess people by. If all a person can do is talk negatively about others, something is very amiss in their life. Be careful of those people who always use their words to project their feelings onto others instead of dealing with themselves.

Faith words will move mountains. I repeat faith words will move every mountain in your life. Sometimes the dreams and visions God gave to you can appear as a mountain. Trust me, writing this book felt like a mountain at various points, but I had to put my mouth to work and let faith arise in my speech.

Through the wrong lens it can feel like the assignment from God will take you out but I am here to remind you that the assignment is to put you back in the race and advance you to the finish line! Kenneth E. Hagin said, *"Faith is always expressed in WORDS. Faith must be released in WORDS through your mouth."*

The enemy has infiltrated the human language with bad words that have the power to kill, steal and destroy. My brothers and sisters in Christ, "yuh big and have sense." Do not let the devil run a train on you with your words because of ignorance.

Jesus' words are life. Hence, they have the ability to create life. It is time that we partner with His words. As stated in the Holy Bible, there is an attack on the word of God. We must be wise because these are our Basic Instructions Before Leaving Earth.

I wondered whoever made us believe that we ought to AGREE with everything in the holy book. That's why Christianity is supposed to be about relationship not religion, because through relationship we will grow in God to understand every word stated in the Bible — whether or not we agree with it.

The problem with the body of Christ is that we believe more in our spiritual leaders than God himself and like that you will always be lead astray. We must admit that some spiritual leaders use the Bible for their own gain and as psychological control over their congregation.

May we break out of this mold and draw near to the word of God that is our sustenance, God words are supposed to be our life line.

Finally, let's examine Elijah and the miracle of fire in 1 Kings 18. This story always blows my mind whenever I read it, because it speaks to God's divine power to bring destruction upon the enemy, and be exalted in the process. In this story we see how the prophet Elijah uses his words, (empowered by his belief in God), to do the unspeakable — the never-before-seen. If this isn't crazy faith, I don't know what is. In verse 27 it says:

"And it came to pass at noon, that Elijah mocked them, and said, Cry aloud: for he is a god; either he is talking, or he is pursuing, or he is in a journey, or peradventure he sleepeth, and must be awaked."

Elijah was able to mock the prophets of Baal because of his assurance and confidence in God. Do you trust the words God has spoken over your life concerning your purpose in him? We need to be like Elijah and mock those against us because we know the God in whom we trust is not a liar but the original truth-teller.

In verses 32 and 33 Elijah did as God commanded in front of his enemies. Its time you begin to live the life of your dreams in front of your haters, somebody say GLOW UP!

Verse 33 stands out for me when it says, *"And he put the wood in order, and cut the bullock in pieces, and laid him on the wood, and said, Fill four barrels with water, and pour it on the burnt sacrifice, and on the wood."*

It likes Sarah Jakes Roberts says, *"Wet wood still burns."* This is so dynamic because naturally wet wood is extremely hard to catch a fire. In fact, it's almost impossible. But that's how God wants our circumstances to appear before He steps on the scene.

So, if you have a situation that seems impossible, do yourself a favour and call upon the name of the Lord. Our God looks at what seems "IMPOSSIBLE" to man, and says "I AM Possible." That right there deserves your AMEN. Use your words and speak to impossibility and watch God make it possible!

Verses 37 and 38 say:

37 Hear me, O LORD, hear me, that this people may know that thou art the LORD God, and that thou hast turned their heart back again.

38 Then the fire of the LORD fell, and consumed the burnt sacrifice, and the wood, and the stones, and the dust, and licked up the water that was in the trench.

We serve a God who answers by fire. Fire contains light and light cannot be hidden. So shall it be with your dreams and visions that God has given to you. They shall all come to pass and silence the mouth of your enemies.

Finally, in verse 39 it says, *"And when all the people saw it, they fell on their faces: and they said, The LORD, he is the God; the LORD, he is the God."* The same people who use their mouth to speak against you and your dreams will thank God for what He has done in and through you.

Again I ask the question: what that mouth do? I want you to view your mouth as an instrument connected to the heart of God, bearing another powerful instrument within it called the tongue. Stop using your mouth to do every other thing except manifesting the life of your dreams with God.

The next time someone asks you this question, tell them, *"Move from here before I bind you up with my words."* Treat your mouth with respect and only fill it with the words of God because anything else will only poison its integrity and degrade your life.

CHAPTER 11:
When Destiny Connects

Destiny can be defined as God's plans and purpose for your life which was conceived long before you were born. In case no one has ever told you this before or maybe you forgot, YOUR LIFE HAS A PURPOSE. You are alive for a reason. Your beating heart symbolizes purpose in motion so go out and live a life that is holy and acceptable unto God.

God has assignments laid out for you to accomplish here on planet earth. God helps us at all moments in our lives especially when we cannot help ourselves. God also delegates the Holy Spirit, angels and people to help us in our time of need. He provides destiny helpers for us, to aid in fulfilling his purpose in our lives. Matthew 7:13-14 (KJV) says:

13 Enter ye in at the strait gate: for wide is the gate, and broad is the way, that leadeth to destruction, and many there be which go in thereat:

14 Because strait is the gate, and narrow is the way, which leadeth unto life, and few there be that find it.

On the broad road your destiny killers and undertakers are waiting for you, so beware of this path. Some of them are so deceptive that they disguise themselves as destiny helpers. This is where godly discernment comes in. For example, you may have a so-called friend under pretense whose assignment is to keep you from maximizing your potential.

The Bible teaches us that narrow is the way that leads to eternal life with Christ Jesus. On this path, your destiny helpers have been strategically planted and are awaiting your arrival. I once heard a pastor say that nothing in life happens by coincidence. It's either divinely orchestrated by God or demonically orchestrated by the Devil. Which kind of orchestration is happening in your life?

Let's examine the story of the Centurion man in Luke 7:1-10. He had an appointment with Destiny and didn't even realise it — a full-on collision with the Son of God.

I marvel at verse 7 which says, *"Wherefore neither thought I myself worthy to come unto thee: but say in a word, and my servant shall be healed."* Now I want us to observe Jesus' response to this in verse 9, *"When Jesus heard these things, he marvelled at him, and turned him about, and said unto the people that followed him, I say unto you, I have not found so great faith, no, not in Israel."*

This man was walking in such great faith that he only needed Jesus to send him ONE WORD. I believe that God has given me this assignment to encourage you and I want you to grab at least one word from this book. Sometimes even in our praying and fasting, we need to ask God for a word. When He gives you that one word, believe it and run with it. Jesus is always amazed at great faith because faith comes by hearing the word of God.

The Bible also says that the word was God, so Faith is the heart of God. When our faith in God rises, it connects to His heart and He responds accordingly. Consider the woman with the issue of blood who touched the hem of Jesus' garment. It was not her physical touch that caught His attention. No, her faith touched His heart and He had an obligation to respond to her need.

The enemy is on assignment to kill, steal and destroy your faith in God. Stay focused on God because you don't know when the tide will turn in your favor — when your destiny will connect with your purpose and lead to your breakthrough.

The Bible says in Psalms 42:7 (KJV) that deep calls unto deep, the deep things of God are calling unto the deep things in your life. Exodus 14:13 (KJV) says:

"And Moses said unto the people, Fear ye not, stand still, and see the salvation of the LORD, which he will shew to you to day: for the Egyptians whom ye have seen to day, ye shall see them again no more for ever."

It's time for you to stop being fearful, stand still and watch God work it all out for you. It's not of matter of IF but a matter of WHEN. Whatever enemy is harassing you right now from this very moment they are being removed from your life in every direction. STAND STILL. As your destiny begins to connect, you will experience a 360 turnaround. This is considered a full rotation — complete. A turnaround is characterized by positive, drastic and evident change.

To experience this you must:

1. Have a strong desire for a turnaround. (How badly do you want it?)

2. Have strong faith for a turnaround. It is your faith in God that will birth this turnaround even in the midst of turmoil.

3. Take a bold step of faith for a turnaround. You need to take an active step of faith through obedience to God's word. You don't know what you can do until you make a move.

4. Wait for your turnaround. No matter how long it takes, you must wait for your turnaround because you turn is coming, don't be discouraged because it seems like everyone else is prospering but YOU.

It is God's grace that will allow this completion to be made. Let's take a look at the story of Naaman and how he experienced a 360 breakthrough. 2 Kings 5:1 tells us that Naaman was a man of valor, but he had a limitation — leprosy. Some of you have great potential within you but it is locked up by your limitations (physical, spiritual or emotional).

In those days lepers were considered unclean and treated as outcasts. I once read that whenever they were out in public and an individual not suffering from leprosy was coming in their direction, they had to ring a bell and shout "unclean." Imagine having to live a life like this but truth is some of you are in this state where you have allowed your past to dictate your future and as a result stagnate your destiny.

I declare that is being reversed right now, in Jesus' name! Declare this with me: *I shall lay hold of my destiny in Christ Jesus and nothing will ever stop me from attaining it.* The Bible did say that the gates of hell shall not prevail against the church so as God's church, why are you allowing the attacks of the enemy to prevail against you?

Naaman really desired a turnaround in his body but let's see what he does when presented with the instructions for a breakthrough. In verse ten it says, *"And Elisha sent a messenger unto him, saying, Go and wash in Jordan seven times, and thy flesh shall come again to thee, and thou shalt be clean."* Now take a look at his response in verses eleven and twelve which read:

11 But Naaman was wroth, and went away, and said, Behold, I thought, He will surely come out to me, and stand, and call on the name of the LORD his God, and strike his hand over the place, and recover the leper.

12 Are not Abana and Pharpar, rivers of Damascus, better than all the waters of Israel? may I not wash in them, and be clean? So he turned and went away in a rage.

Naaman responded like many of us do to God when He gives us the instruction for our breakthrough. Many times, we judge the vessel, strategy or instrument that God wants to use to bless us. How many of you are locked out of your turnaround because the instructions don't sound like what you expected? What happens when God's instructions hit differently than expected?

Naaman was focused on the external appearance of the river. He knew that it was not physically clean. He even questioned why God didn't choose a better river for him to dip into.

Moreover, God required him to dip seven times? I believe that at this point it was pride that was holding him back. He was more concerned with how it would look for a man of valor to degrade himself by dipping in that water.

But thank God for Destiny Helpers, in verse 13 which reads, *"And his servants came near, and spake unto him, and said, My father, if the prophet had bid thee do some great thing, wouldest thou not have done it? how much rather then, when he saith to thee, Wash, and be clean?"*

Just like Naaman, I pray that your destiny helpers will arise in purpose at the point of your breakthrough. They were able to convince Naaman to obey the instructions of God through his man servant the prophet Elisha. Verse 14 reads: *"Then went he down, and dipped himself seven times in Jordan, according to the saying of the man of God: and his flesh came again like unto the flesh of a little child, and he was clean."*

Naaman was able to receive an immediate turnaround at the fulfillment of the instructions given. Some of you may not have a second chance like Naaman to have a change of heart. My encouragement to you is be sharp. Stay ready and focused so you can lay hold of your breakthrough when that moment presents itself to you. The same water that looked unclean was prophetically blessed when God placed His hand upon it. God's hand is already upon your life and the situation so trust him even when it seems crazy and wild.

I must also bring your attention to one more thing about this story which is that the instruction said seven times. Seven speaks of divine completion. It also speaks of perseverance and determination. Sometimes we have to keep on doing a particular thing to get the kind of results we need. Whether it be praying, reading your Bible or fasting regularly. It may be losing some friends or being intentional about your time on the internet.

Just know that there is purpose in the wait. If Naaman had only dipped five or six times and stopped, he still would not have received his turnaround so don't think you can take a shortcut to your breakthrough. It would only end in great disappointment for you. God's command needs to be obeyed in full with all your heart and strength.

360 is the level where God superimposes His plans on your life, where situations must bend or break to reflect God's will, where systems and protocol break in your favor. When your eyes are set on God, you can discern the vessel He will use to bless you in spite of its appearance. Your destiny is waiting to connect you from where you are to where you belong. Hurry up so that you don't miss the ride because the view is always best at the TOP!

CHAPTER 12:
The Power of Passion

I think it's quite fitting to end my book with such a powerful chapter because When God first gives us a dream, it is in its potential state, like potential energy stored up within us. But when we begin to move in accordance with the dream through faith, it begins to become a reality, like kinetic energy. The enemy's plan is to stagnate your dreams in their potential form. But by the grace of God, may all your dreams come to pass, as they are established in the heavens.

A quick Google search tells us that *passion* is "a feeling of intense enthusiasm or compelling desire towards someone or something." *Passion* can also be defined as "spiritual enthusiasm." With this knowledge, which level is your spiritual enthusiasm at?

Reverend Lucy Natasha, a mighty woman of God, made some interesting points on the power of passion in her sermon, *Principles of Kingdom Billionaires Mindset.* I would like to expand on those points:

1. Passion is the vehicle that drives vision

When you are passionate, it motivates you to go after your dreams. Even in the face of adversity, you have the will power to persist. May you begin to persist, in the name of Jesus.

2. Do what you are passionate about

In my lifetime I have seen too many people work at jobs that are not fulfilling to them, and they choose to stay in those jobs for years, decades even, because of a paycheck. I can safely say that is not God's portion for you. God doesn't want us to merely go through life, but to experience it in all its joys and sorrows. It is time to devise an action plan and begin doing those things that evoke passion and fulfillment within you.

3. Your passion is appointed to your purpose

Why we are here, is a question we oftentimes contemplate and wrestle with. I encourage you to spend some time in quiet reflection with God, through fasting and praying. He will make this clear to you. When you find your purpose, it will be the thing that keeps your spirit alive. It will make you happy to wake up in the morning. It will make you appreciative of what you have the opportunity to do. There is no way you can be both purposeful and passionless in an area at the same time. It is your passion that informs your purpose.

4. Success follows vision

When you have your dreams all mapped out, it is then very important to plan in detail to the best of your ability. Map out each step. Factor in obstacles, but don't stop until you see that dream in its fullness. When the vision becomes clear, success is inevitable because you will begin to operate strategically. Anything we consistently work hard on, will surely lead to success.

5. Passion is the energy of vision

Passion is the fuel that keeps the vision burning. Even if life's obstacles try to quench it, your passion shall not be quenched. I remember facing so many challenges while pursuing my Bachelor's degree, that every semester I would consider withdrawing from the program or applying for a leave of absence. In those moments, it was my passion that reenergized me and motivated me to keep on going and look at me now. I am here.

6. You can turn your passion into your source of income

Sometimes God calls us into certain industries that seems and feels like barren land, but God knows best. Stay faithful in that place, remain obedient to the instructions and watch God bring payment through your passion! Teaching has always been my passion since childhood. I can reflect on my life and see how that passion led to improved financial situation. There were times when I had several teaching jobs at the same time.

It was not me of myself, but the passion God put in me, that led me to realms of unexpected opportunities and allowed me to get paid. If you can't see yourself making enough money for your sustenance in the area you are called to serve, please wipe your eyes and look again. Maybe you are looking at the situation through the wrong lens. God would never lead you to a place to die — He is too merciful and good.

7. Passion turns ordinary into extraordinary

I am a testimony to this fact. When you are truly passionate about what you do, it is evident in the quality of work that you produce. Some people 'pretend passion.' That is, they operate under the guise that they love what they do, when most times their service or contribution is all for show and recognition. A person who is truly passionate does not do it for the recognition. Passion leads to excellence, more so godly excellence.

As a child of God, you should be an example at your job because of how you conduct yourself and your business. You should lead with love and integrity. Your passion should overflow into every area of your job. Additionally, passionate people carry a glow that cannot be denied. People always ask me why I am always smiling and happy. I often take the opportunity to remind them that when you are fulfilling your God-given-mandate, peace, love and joy are your portion. I am taking all that God has given.

8. Passion causes you to place the extra touch

When you are passionate, you automatically become intentional about what you are doing. You naturally go above and beyond what is required of you. This speaks to my approach to the work of God. Many times I am the last one to leave church. I would always diligently lock up and do other mundane tasks, knowing it is my service to God. At one point I was juggling teaching Sunday school, running youth ministry, directing the worship team and being an assistant pastor. It was my passion and the fact that I was doing all in obedience to God that enabled me to do all in excellence.

9. Your passion will distinguish you

Passion will cause you to be singled out from the multitude. I remember when I was selected to be one of the teachers of English at Good Hope Secondary school, I was publicly acknowledged by the Region Education Officer. I smiled because I know that it was my passion and diligence that distinguished me in that moment.

Volunteering at the Guyana Learning Channel really broadened my horizon as an educator, and sent my name abroad, so to speak. As my quality of work and passion set me apart, persons began to respect me more as an educator. I received an outpouring of love from parents, students and fellow teachers. As my diligence in pursuing my passion brought me recognition, your passion can do the same for you. Do not let fear or criticism keep you from being all you can be.

10. You will be known in the world for your passion

Passion has the ability to make you very impactful and this is the part of you that can never be replaced. Your impact is your legacy that lives on even after your physical death. I want you to think of five people that inspire you the most. Now that you have done that, I want you to know their inspiration on your life is as a result of their pursuit of their passion. Imagine if they weren't passionate! that would be one less person who inspired you!

11. Your passion will make people connect you to something

I am known as different things in different arenas, depending on who you ask. If it is from the educational fraternity, they will tell you I am Sir Jared, because of my zest for teaching. If it is from my church circle, they will say I am Brother Jared, because when it comes to God I go HARD. Your passion will cause people to see and respect you for the thing that is unique to you. So, stop fighting it and start embracing what God is doing in you through your passion.

12. Passionate people don't give up

Listen to me and listen to me carefully: you are not a quitter. Giving up is not your portion. I need you to claim that now. Even if you don't feel that way now, start speaking it over yourself and your passion. Passionate people find new and creative ways and means of making their dreams happen. They understand that valley moments may arise, but only to teach a lesson — never to deter success.

There is a song I love to sing at church which says,

> *I am determined to hold on to the end,*
> *Jesus is with me on him I can depend*
> *For I know I have salvation, way down in my soul,*
> *I am determined to hold on to the end.*
> *Hold on, hold on, hoo, hoo, hoo,*
> *Hold on, hold on, hold on, hold on*
> *I am determined to hold on to the End.*

Hold on my brothers and sisters. I am rooting for you, but most importantly the whole Trinity is rooting for your success. They already see how your story ends, and it ends in victory! Start rejoicing now!

13. Passion brings influence

The right people will want to be around you. They will find your passion inspiring and will want to stay as close to you as possible, knowing there is so much to learn. Your tribe will not try to compete with your influence, but will do their best to build you up, since they too want to see you continuously thriving in your passion.

14. If you lose your passion, you lose your place

The minute you let go of your passion, it becomes quite evident in your output. It will also diminish what you have achieved through it. It is your passion that keeps you in place. I want to use this opportunity to say to you: even if many people don't recognize your passion and potential, stay true and faithful to it. In due season, you will gain the right recognition for your hard work. All attention isn't good attention, take it from me.

Revelation 2:4-5 (NIV) says,

"4 Yet I hold this against you: You have forsaken the love you had at first. 5 Consider how far you have fallen! Repent and do the things you did at first. If you do not repent, I will come to you and remove your lampstand from its place."

What do you do when you have lost your passion?

1.   Practice getting it back! 1 Corinthians 15:57-58 says,

"57 But thank God! He gives us victory over sin and death through our Lord Jesus Christ.

58 So, my dear brothers and sisters, be strong and immovable. Always work enthusiastically for the Lord, for you know that nothing you do for the Lord is ever useless."
We must be intentional about regaining our passion, because it is our spiritual enthusiasm that fuels us to keep on going.

In 1 Samuel 17: 45-46 (NLT) says,

"45 David replied to the Philistine, "You come to me with sword, spear, and javelin, but I come to you in the name of the LORD of Heaven's Armies—the God of the armies of Israel, whom you have defied. 46 Today the LORD will conquer you, and I will kill you and cut off your head. And

then I will give the dead bodies of your men to the birds and wild animals, and the whole world will know that there is a God in Israel!"

I constantly ask myself where David as a young man got this passion from and I came to realise three things:

(a) He trusted God daily.
(b) Walked with God daily.
(c) Worship with God daily.

Maybe if you started doing these three things daily as he did, your passion will be rekindled. For some of you, your passion needs re-centering. I have observed that we lose our passion when we take our eyes off of our calling and placed them on our comfort. David sinned against God by the act he committed with Bathsheba, and he tried to cover his wicked acts.

Psalm 51:10-12 (NIV) says,

*"10 Create in me a pure heart, O God,
and renew a steadfast spirit within me.*

11 Do not cast me from your presence

or take your Holy Spirit from me.

12 Restore to me the joy of your salvation
and grant me a willing spirit, to sustain me."

David was able to remedy his situation by doing what he proclaimed in the verses above — 1) by making a public declaration to God and 2) by being consistent in his pursuit of holy living. I charge you to declare these words over your life each day to the Lord, and watch your passion find your address again.

BEWARE OF THE FOLLOWING PASSION STEALERS

(i) Lust- Ephesians 4:19 NIV-
    "Having lost all sensitivity, they have given themselves over to sensuality so as to indulge in every kind of impurity, and they are full of greed."

(ii) Fear- 1 John 4:18 NIV-
    "There is no fear in love. But perfect love drives out fear, because fear has to do with punishment. The one who fears is not made perfect in love."

(iii)Resentment- Job 5:2 NLT-
    "Surely resentment destroys the fool, and jealousy kills the simple."

In closing, I encourage you to

—Dare to live your heart's desire:

Psalm 37:46 NIV:

"Take delight in the LORD,
and he will give you the desires of your heart."

Colossians 3:23 NIV:

"Whatever you do, work at it with all your heart, as
working for the Lord, not for human masters."

—Depend on God to Power your passion:

Psalm 37:4a NIV:

"Take delight in the LORD,
and he will give you the desires of your heart."

Psalm 37:23-24 NIV:

"23 The LORD makes firm the steps
of the one who delights in him;

24 though he may stumble, he will not fall,
for the LORD upholds him with his hand."

It is by the Grace of God that I am. He meets all of my needs and I know that He has kept me through thick and thin, and will continue to keep me. Faith is the key that unlocks the grace of God. It is this grace that has allowed me to find my voice through truth, honor and love. With this book I have found my voice, my identity. I stand fully in acceptance of my whole self, as I embrace what God does next in my life.

For by grace are ye saved through faith; and that not of yourselves: it is the gift of God: Not of works, lest any man should boast.

Ephesians 2:8-9

ABOUT THE AUTHOR

Jared Nicholas Demarco McPhoy is an English teacher at Annandale Secondary school in Guyana, which is located in the continent of South America. He has been an Educator for over four years and has attained his Bachelors Degree in Education- English (Secondary) from the University of Guyana. He credits his teaching experience for his ability to connect with people of different races and creeds.

He has served in his home church from 14 years old and has functioned in several capacities such as Assistant Pastor, Sunday school teacher, and Youth Ministry and Worship Director. His experience in ministry that has guided him through his relationship with God and himself.

He was born in the Mining town of Linden, Moved to Parika, and then to Vryheid's Lust where he spent most of his life. His book will stir up a series of emotions within you as you read, and he shares about his relationship with family, friends and church community. You will laugh, cry and most importantly, feel motivated to get up and go after your dreams.

Keep up with Jared on Instagram @forever_bless98

REFERENCES

Dream - King James Dictionary -. StudyLight.org. (n.d.). Retrieved September 8, 2022, from https://www.studylight.org/dictionaries/eng/kjd/d/dream.html

Emily Dickinson Lexicon. Emily Dickinson Lexicon - DRAWN-BUT'TER – DREAM'ER. (n.d.). Retrieved September 8, 2022, from https://edl.byu.edu/webster/D/193